# Barefoot, Bloodied and Bruised

*The amazing story of Louisiana six-man football*

## Coach Barrett Murphy

**Barefoot, Bloodied and Bruised**
Copyright © 2014 Barrett Murphy

ISBN: 9-781499-692655

Printed in the United States.
Available from Amazon.com and other retail outlets.

# Acknowledgements

There are many people who made this book possible. First and foremost is my wife Jennie, who tolerated my obsession for almost four years and was still supportive and good-natured enough to help out with the preparation of the manuscript. My two sons, Andrew Brett Murphy and Greg Murphy and my granddaughter Gabrielle Murphy also contributed in various ways to completing the project.

Amanda Hines spent many hours transcribing interviews and DVDs. Many thanks to Howard Rankin who did a great job capturing the spirit of the times and the stories in his writing and editing. Very special thanks to Jack Joubert, renowned local sports artist who created the artwork on the cover.

The book would not have been possible without the contributions of all the wonderful people from the great state of Louisiana who submitted memories, newspaper articles and great pictures from their private collections.

My deepest appreciation and thanks goes to the following people who willingly gave their time and effort to make the book possible. Collectively, they had the memory of the story of six-man football in Louisiana. This book simply wouldn't have been possible without them.

Iota: Dr. Gibson Miller

Brusly: L.J. Dupuy

Port Barre: Mr. William Duplechin, Principal

St. Gabriel: L.G. Hoffman

St Gabriel and White Castle: Herb Hernandez, Coach

Denham Springs: Robert Graves, Gene Clark – Walker correspondant for the "The Denham Springs – Livingston Parish News" article "1946 Denham Springs Game is Replayed"

McKowen: Lucille Priddy Fulcker, Sonny Harris

Woodland: Chris Davis

Sacred Heart of Ville Platte: The Honorable John Saunders (District Court Judge, State of Louisiana); Bobby Soileau, Coach; Articles & information from *Bonnes Nouvelles* newspaper, Ville Platte, La.

Dutchtown: Conrad Braud, *Dutchtown School; History & Community 1858-1966* by Harriet Babin Miller

Rayne: Charles Sidney Stutes, Tommy Petitjohn

Clinton: Mrs. Alberta Williams

Basile: Ernie Duplechin, Coach; Mrs. Dolores Duplechin

Bell City: Sonny Arceneaux, Clarence Theriot, Coach

Creole: J.C. Reina, Coach

Livonia: Jimmy Walker

Golden Meadow: Eston Pitre, Brent St. Germain, Sports Editor, The Courier and Daily Comet, Houma and Thibodeaux, Louisiana

Larose Cut Off: Numa Braud, Sidney Triche

Referees: Levi Dabadie, Gerald Didier, Allen Buddy LeBlanc

Other contributors include:

Smiley Anders, The Advocate, Baton Rouge, La
Tommy Murphy
Barry Spears
Al Tricuit
Louisiana High School Athletic Association
Tom Conti
Stafford Chenevert, of New Roads, La., Pointe Coupe Banner newspaper
Vision Communications, Houma, La.
Daily Iberian, New Iberia, La.

Many thanks to you all!

# Table of Contents

# FOREWORD

The stories in this book are but a sampling and an attempt to present the true history of six-man football in the state of Louisiana. The book is based on real life interviews that were conducted over the past four years. I traveled around the state of Louisiana interviewing individuals who had played the game or were involved in the game in some capacity, i.e. administrators, coaches, players, cheerleaders, coaches wives, referees, managers, etc. Actually, I grabbed anyone I could find who had played or knew about six-man football in the state!

As I traveled, I was amazed at the number of people who were not aware that the Six-Man Football Game was played for nearly three decades in Louisiana. This window was closed for so many years. Now the window is opened for people to see what these great folks did for Louisiana High School football! These people were the foundation for many of the eleven-man programs of today. (Time is of the essence because many of these players are gone and the ones still here are in later stages of life.) The players, coaches, principals, and teachers are truly legends in their own right. It is most important to respect the past. They played, they vanished, and many are gone to the 80 x 40 field in the big sky! We cannot let them be forgotten!

Coach Barrett Murphy

Spring 2014

# Six-Man Introduction and Rules

Stephen Epler, a high school coach in Chester, Nebraska, started six-man football in 1934 as a way for small schools to participate in football during the great Depression. Texas, with a strong football tradition and many rural schools, adopted the sport and the first game was played there in 1936. Many southern states took the game up. Currently, Texas has at least 195 schools playing six-man, Florida 32, Colorado 23, Alabama 8, and the sport is played in Iowa, Idaho, Nebraska, Wyoming, and in New Mexico.

## Rules

- Six players.

- 15 yards for a first down to be made in four plays.

- The field is 40 yards wide, 80 yards long and the end line is 10 yards from the goal line, making the field a total of 100 yards long.

- Goalposts are 25 feet apart and the crossbar is 9 feet from the ground.

- A field goal is worth 4 points.

- After TD kick worth 2 points.

- Quarters are 10 minutes long.

- Game called if team is ahead 45 points at half or at any time during the second half – so called 'Slaughter' or 'Mercy' rule.

- All players eligible to receive a forward pass.

- Only free kick is the kick-off from the thirty-yard line.

- A forward pass that does not pass the line of scrimmage in flight is considered a backward pass.

- A clear pass must be made by the receiver of the snap before the ball can be advanced past the line of scrimmage by running. Clear pass is not necessary before a kick or forward pass.

- A clear pass is one that is thrown by the receiver of the snap and which travels a clearly visible distance through the air and then touches a player other than the passer.

- A fumble, backward pass or clear pass may be recovered and advanced by the defensive team, even after the ball has touched the ground.

- At least three players of the offensive team must be at the line of scrimmage when the ball is snapped.

Some rule changes were implemented for the 1945 season.

- Substitutes no longer need to report to the referee or umpire. They must report to the scorer.

- Any kick which crosses the receiver's goal line becomes dead and is considered a touchback.

- Penalty for intentionally discarding headgear is now 5 yards.

- Any kick from scrimmage touched by the receivers and beyond the scrimmage line and recovered by the kickers is an automatic first down, regardless of whether that recovery is behind or beyond the scrimmage line.

- The kick-off is now the only kick-off in six man football. All kick-offs including those following a safety, start from the thirty-yard line.

- Everything else is the same as eleven-man.

In Ray Duncan's book *Six Man Football*, there is a wealth of information about the game, everything from training, tactics, medical treatment, the setting of standards for players to the administrative cost of fielding a team.

On the subject of minimum rules for the players, the author suggests the following:

- You should work hard
- You should get nine hours of sleep a night
- You should not drink
- You should not smoke
- You should not have dates during the week.

When you read this book you'll find out how well the players of the era conformed to those standards.

One of the virtues of six-man was that it didn't require as many resources as fielding an eleven-man team. There were far fewer players, thus uniforms and maintenance were less.

In his book, Duncan calculates that uniforms for a twenty-man squad would cost $365, Balls $25.50, and training supplies $16.75, for a total of $407.25. But he adds that doesn't include the cost of the field. However, he suggests that, "the goal posts can be made and installed with very little expense and down markers and chain can be made in the school workshop." He also notes that the cost of transportation and officials vary.

Six-man was considered a safer game, as there was very rarely gang tackling, most of the plays really being one-on-one, and the field far more open than in eleven-man.

In the following pages you will read how each school coped with these challenges, what the game meant to the players, the schools and their communities, and why this sport of the World War II era should never be forgotten.

---

# A Lost Bus, a Shotgun and a Championship

## Dutchtown Eagles

It's the fall of 1942 in the Louisiana parish of Ascension, about 60 miles west of New Orleans. The world is embroiled in a horrendous conflict that will affect the lives of almost everyone gathered on this Friday afternoon. Not that they would know that at the time, and even if some of them thought about the uncertain future, today was a chance to escape the specter of war. For this afternoon was something special, something to tell your children and your grandchildren about.

These were the days of hard work and simple pleasures. For the students of Dutchtown High School – graduating class of about 50 but no graduation ceremony – there wasn't the vast spectrum of sports and school organized activities that their grandchildren would come to expect. Heck, there wasn't even a school cafeteria until 1946. So it was something really special when the 1949 Dutchtown Eagles six-man football team made it to the championship game against Jeanerette.

Kermit Braud, son of the Dutchtown High Principal admits that, "In those days we didn't know much about football. I was interested in boxing. It was the days of Joe Louis and Max Schmelling. We had a battery radio at grandpa's house and my neighbors and uncles would come, and we'd sit up on the hill listening to boxing matches." In fact, Dutchtown had a boxing team and the coach, Mr. Conrad, would watch the inevitable fights at recess and turn them into scouting opportunities.

Kermit has the distinction of riding to football practice on a horse and running home through the woods to his grandpa's house immediately afterwards. There were no well-equipped gymnasiums, no sophisticated workout equipment, no finely tuned exercise regimen, and in many ways, no need for any of that. This was 30 years before the term 'aerobics' was coined -- or needed to be. The boys were already in good physical condition.

Kermit recalls, "If you let your grandfather follow you and tell you what to do, you're going to stay in pretty good shape. We opened drains with a shovel. We threw bales of hay over the side of the wagon. We made hay by hand; there were no tractors. I plowed with a mule when I was 12 and the plow itself must have weighed a hundred pounds."

In fact, farm work was such an essential part of a teenage boy's life in Dutchtown that some potential football stars weren't allowed to play because they were needed at the farm.

"Some of the families and some of the daddies didn't let their sons play football because they had to work in the farm. We all had to pick strawberries, I cut sugarcane for a neighbor, and it was very important that all the boys worked in the field," recalls Kermit.

Some families simply didn't want their sons to play football at all. Benjamin Franklin Delaune, who featured on later Dutchtown teams, recalls that his father wasn't happy about him playing – at first. But things changed after he made his first appearance for the team.

"After that first game, Henry, my brother, brought him down to Dutchtown and he watched me play. He wouldn't miss a game after that for nothing in the world. When you said, 'football,' he was ready!" remembers Ben Delaune.

Many things were different back then. The team traveled to road games on uncomfortable buses with no air conditioning and long benches. The students traveled on buses, too. But things didn't always work out the way they were meant to when on the road.

These were the days long before cell phones and GPS. Both would have been useful on one fateful road trip. Rocky Frederic, the water boy and then equipment manager, recalls one rainy afternoon traveling to Jackson, home of the McKowen Rebels. The driver got lost and arrived at half-time, only to discover that the game had been cancelled.

Lawrence Leblanc, played on the victorious '49 team and also played basketball. He recalled a trip to French Settlement where he and the rest of the visiting team had to run a dozen pigs out of their dressing room!

Lawrence LeBlanc wasn't a big guy either and epitomized the balance needed for successful six-man. There were big guys who could block and small guys that could run like the wind. Lawrence was one of the members of the 1949 team and he recalls that of the 23 players on that team, 11 of them are no longer alive. And he remembers running for his own life during one memorable game against Jackson.

"It had rained and rained, and then rained some more. I picked up a fumble and started running towards their goal line. They had this big, tough guy who must have been 200 pounds chasing me and I was maybe 140 pounds soaking wet, which I was at the time. He had me running so fast because I didn't want him catching up with me and landing on me. I ran it all the way in for a touchdown."

Some of the action on the field was more unconventional. Every man on offense was an eligible receiver, which lent itself well to an aerial attack. Kermit Braud, the Principal's horse-riding son, played as an end. His favorite play was called "snake in the grass." Basically, this play required Kermit to effectively hide amongst the spectators that were crowded on the sidelines, then run back on the field at the appropriate time to catch a touchdown pass. This worked well because despite being strong, Kermit was a mere 142 pounds and could be easily lost in the sideline commotion.

"I'd stay and hide behind a spectator and then when they centered the ball I'd run on the field and, of course, I was easy to find. I was the only one out there! I remember our quarterback Tony Burshee throwing me a touchdown which helped us beat local rival Gonzales," says Braud.

Six-man didn't require complicated offensive sets. There was no wishbone and the only shotguns were down on the farm. Kermit recalls the time his grandpa actually used his double barrel. His grandma had gone to collect the washing before the rains came and got spurred by a rooster while lifting the sheets off the line. She was uncharacteristically quiet when she came in with the washing and grandpa asked her what was wrong. When she told him, he took the shotgun and took care of the rooster.

"Something died every time he picked up the gun," says Kermit.

Some aspects of the games played back then are timeless and would be recognizable today. There was, for example, a tremendous school spirit, characterized by game day pep rallies led by the cheerleaders.

Justine Brunson, wife of the revered coach, W.C. Brunson, recalls, "We always had a pep rally before a game, and the girls did all of the activities, but the boys would show up, too."

Sometimes the excitement got a little out of hand during the game, too. During one trip to Buras, there seemed to be too much excitement in the crowd. Kermit Braud explains.

"We were playing in Buras and it was right after the orange season and all the people in the bleachers were drinking orange wine and betting on the game. There was some commotion on the sidelines and fights were breaking out."

Coach Brunson's half time talk ended with very specific instructions. Fearing an escalation of the fighting and an outbreak of unnecessary roughness, the coach told his team, "When the whistle blows, y'all run and get in the school bus because we're going to have some trouble here." And that's exactly what the boys did after defeating the hometown team. "So as soon as the last whistle blew, we all ran to the bus in our uniforms, no shower or anything," says Kermit. But it wasn't as if the boys missed out on a post game meal. Lawrence LeBlanc recalls the fact that there were no pre- or post- game meals.

"You weren't going to be fed on the road or before the game, or after the game, so you had to eat before school and then wait until you got home to get your next meal," LeBlanc recalls.

**Coach Brunson**
William Charles Brunson shares part of his name with a movie legend who generally played a tough guy who took the law into his own hands. On the contrary, Coach W.C. Brunson was not Hollywood. He didn't do drama or bravado – he didn't need to. The coach was as real as a man can get, adored by his players, principled, unwavering, fair, inspirational. He brought to the six-man league and to his school another timeless characteristic of successful sports teams and winners generally – leadership.

W.C. was a shining example of his greatest generation. There was no egotism, simply a commitment to what was right, respect for everyone including his players, and service to his country.

The coach was born in Eunice, Louisiana in St. Landry parish. He was educated at University of Southwest Louisiana, USL (now the University of Louisiana at Lafayette), and was recruited to teach the seventh grade in Dutchtown. Principal Harry Braud wanted a male teacher and W.C. got the call. The salary was $72 per month for the nine months of school. Teachers didn't get paid when school wasn't in session.

As he was from out of town, W.C. stayed at the Teacherage, a big house set aside for non-local teachers. W.C. lived in a front room, while Justine, another teacher shared a room with a female colleague. That was in 1937, when W.C. first arrived. Two years later, W.C. and Justine took over a room at the back of the house and a kitchen area after they were married. It was where they raised their children, Cheryl and Janis.

Justine describes her husband as, "very calm, always calm and he never got excited. He believed in what he was doing for sure. He was a person people liked. He didn't fuss."

To say that people liked him is an understatement.

B.F. Delaune said about his former coach, "I loved him to death. He was just a good person to get along with." He recalls the coach telling him, "B.F., I want you to be tough and mean." So B.F. got out there and was tough and mean.

"I'd go in there with my elbows because at that time you could block with your elbows and that was my weapon of blocking. That's the way we played ball back then. You got out there and you fought. It's a rough game and I just had fun doing it."

Rocky Frederic, the water-boy, says, "Coach Brunson was a very smart man and he was a very smart coach."

Typically, the most athletic kids played the whole game on both offense and defense. However, in one game against St. Amant, coach changed things up after heading to the locker room down 24-0. He started alternating his first and second teams to preserve energy and keep his players as fresh as possible in the afternoon heat. After the second team defensive unit held St. Amant scoreless in their first possession of the second-half, the first team offense marched down the field for their first score. This established a pattern and Dutchtown ran out winners, 42-24.

Rocky is proud of his association with coach Brunson. Being the water boy and the equipment manager, he spent a lot of time around the coach.

"Because of my association with Mr. Brunson and the football team, he got me a scholarship to LSU, all expenses paid. That's what he did for me," says Rocky who wrote this poem as testimony to the fun football years at Dutchtown.

Football Daze
By O.J. "Rocky" Frederic

"It's that time of year again,
And it happens each fall,
When hale and hearty young men
Get ready for high school football.
It makes me remember that year
In nineteen hundred and forty-seven
When I had to get ready my gear,
And it was six, instead of eleven.
That year I realized my dream,
To be part of the football team.
It was rough and tough but I stuck it out,
I learned what football was all about.
I remember the excitement, roar of the fans,
The cheerleaders in front of the stands
And there was one cheer and student yell,
That I'll always remember very well.
I'll pass it on to you, and you will see,
Why this one cheer meant so much to me.
It was" "Rocky, Rocky, he's our joy!
He's our darling water boy!"

Lawrence Leblanc recalls, "The coach and principal Mr. W.C. Brunson, was a very fine man and coach. He taught us a lot about being good sports and doing what you need to do to be a good team player."

Lawrence and a couple of other team mates, like quarterback Bobby Peno, actually had two senior years because a twelfth grade was added in 1949. After school, Lawrence served in the Marines for 9 years.

And so to the 1942 championship game.

Jeanerette took an early lead but Dutchtown combined an aerial attack and end runs to overtake them and win the game 31-29.

Cheryl, the coach's daughter, recalls that the mix of small, fast players like Kermit Braud, and some big blockers, made the running game hard to stop. She recalls "The size of the Dutchtown boys made their end run successful because of the interference they could give."

It was only a few months later, that the distant but unsettling war came closer to home. Like many coaches of that time, W.C. joined the service, in his case the Navy, where he served before retuning home in 1945. He went back to Dutchtown, became the principal and continued coaching, winning another championship, in 1949, the last year of six-man football at Dutchtown. Eleven-man was introduced the following year under a new coach "Dock" Dement.

Lawrence Leblanc played in the 1949 championship game and recalls hearing that his opponents, Delcambre, were boasting that they were going to stomp those Dutchtown boys.

"That didn't go down too well with us," says Lawrence.

You can't imagine it going down too well with Coach Brunson either, who probably turned the taunting into motivation for his team. And so, in his last game in charge of the Dutchtown six-man team, Coach Brunson fittingly lifted the championship again, with a 42-12 win, which was reported like this in the Daily Iberian on December 9, 1949.

"The Dutchtown Eagles copped the state six-man football here last night when they handed the Delcambre Panthers a decisive 42-12 drubbing."

"Dutchtown rolled up an impressive 30-12 lead at halftime and coasted to their victory. Owen Braud and Bobby Peno stood out on offense and defense for the Eagles."

"Braud scored three touchdowns for the Eagles."

And then, six-man was gone from Dutchtown.

Dutchtown's State Champions, 1942

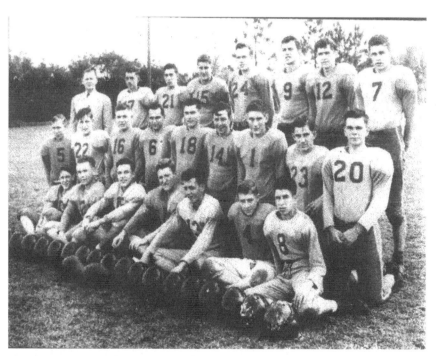

Dutchtown's State Champions, 1949

# The Band, Mentoring, and Instant Encouragement

## Port Barre Red Devils

Port Barre is in St Landry Parish, Louisiana, an area of 1.1 square miles with a few hundred homes and barely a couple of thousand residents. A small town like Port Barre needs to gets its inspiration, role models, guidance, hope and pride from somewhere. Starting in 1949, the six-man football program helped to provide all those qualities to both the young men who represented the Port Barre High School Red Devils and the community at large.

One value of a six-man program was that it allowed small schools in small towns, like Port Barre, to compete. A school like Port Barre could, with considerable effort, find nineteen students to fill out their roster. At that time, it would have been difficult if not impossible, to find at least twice that number that would be needed to field a somewhat competitive eleven man team. Six-man made fielding a team, and all the benefits that came with it, a possibility.

There were some challenges of competing as a very small school. It required some multi-tasking.

Dr. James Kennison, a hugely influential figure in Port Barre history, recalls the varied roles team members had.

"We had football players who were also in the band. At halftime they would change their gear to a cap that they wore for the band. It was pretty good to see," he recalls.

Kennison himself was versatile. He was fast, very fast. This prompted one of the coaches to take the young James under his wing. The coach was betting that he could turn James into a track star. James's dad was also betting – for a living. A professional gambler probably doesn't provide too much domestic stability.

Kennison recalls a conversation with Coach Bordelon.

"Coach said to me, 'I'm going to make you a track star, but you have to come live with me.' My dad was a professional gambler so I said, 'That would be great.' I lived with him the last year of my school."

That guidance and mentoring helped James develop his natural talent. He had talent.

"I guess one of the better games I had the privilege of playing I scored seven touchdowns against St Eds in Eunice," he recalls.

Coach Bordelon wasn't the only one who had Kennison's best interests at heart.

"I guess the  game of football, especially six-man, got me started in the right direction. When you are a son of a professional gambler, its kind of hard to break those ties sometimes but I did through perseverance and help from the Port Barre High School coaches and Principal Professor Lefleur," says Kennison.

But if the principal could be nurturing, he could also be tough.

"He tended to push people in the right direction. Not that he didn't warm my butt with his belt about every other day, but it was one of those things you just accepted because that's how we were taught how to live," recalls Dr. Kennison.

Upon graduation, Kennison applied to go to the Southern Louisiana Institute of Technical and Liberal Leaning or SLI as it was then known. The college has changed names since then and was called the University of Southwestern Louisiana before becoming part of the state college system in 1999 and is now known as University of Louisiana at Lafayette.

Professor J. Howard Lefleur had helped James get some money for college through what was called a 'legislative scholarship'.

James also tried out for football at SLI.

"Coach Raymond Didier was my coach there. One of the assistant coaches was a guy called Bull McLelland from Crowley. We also had Charlie Peavey as backfield coach and he was quite an athlete and later was an LSU assistant coach with the legendary Charlie Mac of the LSU Fighting Tigers."

Kennison recalls what happened after he tried out.

"Coach Didier called me in and I was ready to be told that I didn't make it. But he offered me a full scholarship! So, I came back and told Professor Lefleur, 'I don't want your GD scholarship.' He said 'What are you talking about?' And I told him I'd got my own but thank you anyway."

"You know I appreciate that because now I'm going to give it to someone else," the professor replied.

James Kennison wasn't the only team member whose life was significantly influenced by playing six-man. Ron Carriere, wasn't a running back as his name might suggest, but was the center.

"I remember coaches Carol Webb and his assistant Gordon Bordelon. They were both fine men but they weren't bashful about working you hard. Football taught me discipline and respect. I would have never done anything to disappoint my coaches," says Ron.

"I don't think I would have amounted to much without that discipline that those men instilled in me. I doubt if I would have gotten a college education or even I cared. It meant everything to me."

"I served in the US army from 1952-54 11th Airborne Division. I earned a parachute badge and earned the National Defense Medal. During my time in army airborne, I made approximately 25 jumps," says Ron.

Although Ron was the center he did occasionally carry the ball, as everyone did in six-man. He describes one play.

"When the tailback got the ball, he ran up and stopped at the center. I had the left end position and came across from the right, picked up the ball from him and went on. We usually gained some pretty good ground with that play. That was play number five, end around, and it brought us a few touchdowns," Ron recalls.

It also led to a memorable moment for Ron.

James Kennison remembers.

"I recall the first touchdown ever made by Port Barre High school. One of my best friends Ronald Carriere scored, but he didn't know he had. Somebody knocked the ball out of this guy's hands in the end zone but he recovered it. When everybody started clapping, we didn't know what had happened, but he had scored the first touchdown in Port Barre's six-man history!"

That first game was played against Arcadia. Port Barre won 20-0, a rare shutout in six-man. The elements might have had something to do with the low scoring game. It had been raining hard all day. This caused a dilemma for Ron Carriere, the scorer of that first ever touchdown.

"It rained cats and dogs, and I didn't know whether to go to school or not. I didn't know whether you played football in the rain," recalls Ron.

Another starter on that first six-man team was Jesse Duplechin.

"Our coaches were serious about practice. When it was hot, we didn't get many water breaks, and when we did we had to swallow salt tablets with them. In the summertime it was always hot and practice was pretty rough. We had to ride bicycles from home to school. Of course, peddling that bicycle helped us get in better shape," recalls Jesse.

Jesse was pretty athletic and active in sports year round.

"I played fast pitch softball, second base, and ran track."

Jesse recalls that the first Port Barre team was very talented, and that talent led to some lopsided scores in the wide-open spaces of the six-man football field.

Jesse recalls one such match-up.

"One of the most memorable games was when we played Arnaudville. We skunked them pretty good by halftime and they just called the game off."

It's unclear how fans would take to the abandonment of a game but James Kennison suggests that at least in Port Barre, the locals weren't too keen on seeing their home town school on the wrong end of the scoreline.

Kennison says, "As far as attendance was concerned, it depended on who we were playing because if it was a team that we figured we could beat, attendance was pretty good. Those times when we didn't have a chance, we didn't have too much of an attendance because they didn't want to see us lose."

The fan facilities were fairly primitive.

"People were pretty friendly. We didn't have any bleachers and people would back up their trucks and sit on the tailgate to watch the game. We did have a concession stand that was always pretty busy."

Opposing teams would occasionally try unusual means to stop the Port Barre athletes.

"One of the teams we played each year was another small school and we suspected that instead of water they were using something else to maybe give them more "encouragement." We used to call alcohol 'instant encouragement,'" Kennison explains.

"And I do think that maybe that's what they had because it was pretty easy for us to score on them and it didn't seem like their faculties were in alignment," recalls Kennison.

The faculties that Kennison are referring to are not the teachers and administrators of the school.

William Duplechin is the current Principal at Port Barre. He is also former coach and past president of Louisiana High School Athletic Association. He is the godson of Jesse, who played on those first six-man teams.

"My father graduated from the school in 1941, and all four of my children graduated from there. Dr. James Kennison was my high school track and football coach and even more my mentor."

"Kennison, Carriere, and my parrain Jesse, were the foundation of the six-man football team at Port Barre. Port Barre, at that time, was a rural school with not many students and not very many athletes. These guys laid the foundation and framework for a solid eleven-man football program," says Duplechin.

"These three guys and their teammates who started six man at Port Barre were my idols. They were young enough, or we were old enough, to know them as young adults, and we looked up to those guys. Those guys were our heroes," says the current Principal.

He believes that Ron, James and Jesse in particular were the mainstays not just of their team but the ones that followed, too.

"We knew very little about the mechanics of football but when we went out to play the game we thought about guys like Dr. Kennison and how courageous they were. They were not very big. Mr. Carriere was a lineman. My parrain, Jesse Duplechin, was a lineman but he was fast. He could almost keep up with Dr. Kennison and he was very fast."

William's connection with six-man runs deeper. The principal who hired him at Delcambre High School was the coach of the six-man team that lost to Dutchtown in the finals.

Donny Perron, who was a coach for 27 years, expresses his admiration and appreciation.

"These guys were pioneers. We hear stories about them and see them in town and we're very proud of what they accomplished and what they started back in the late forties and early fifties."

Perhaps James Kennison sums it up best.

"We were heroes I guess in a way because in six-man, you could vent your feelings and take it out on somebody with headgear on. But that's why I enjoyed the game so much because it was competition, and it teaches you things to get ready for in life."

From left: William Duplechin, present Principal, Jesse Duplechin, James
Kennison, Ronald Carriere, Coach Donnie Perron

# A Trip to China, a Remarkable Comeback
# and Pay Dirt

## Iota Bulldogs

Iota, as you might expect, is a small dot of a town in Acadia Parish in south central Louisiana. Iota wasn't always the name of this 1.3 square miles of land. It was previously known as 'Pointe aux loups' (French for 'Wolves Point'), Cartville and Hodge Town. The population numbers about 1600 residents. It's not the sort of place you would associate with sporting excellence. Yet, remarkably, the Iota Bulldogs not only won the six-man football state championship in the 1954-55 season, they went through their entire thirteen game schedule unbeaten.

Immortality and an unblemished schedule seemed a distant dream when Iota fielded its first six-man team in 1951. The sport was very popular across the state and the leagues were very competitive. In those first couple of years, Iota was often on the wrong end of a lopsided score line.

Adrian Hunt, fullback on the undefeated team, recalls that in the early years, "We'd get beat 73 to nothing, 84 to nothing, scores like that."

So how did this small town team go from embarrassing drubbings to undefeated champions in a couple of years?

Let's start with the coach, Elliott Deville, who was ably assisted by his assistant E.J. Castile. Coach Deville started practices early in preparation for the 1954-55 season. And those practices were tough.

"We started practicing probably the first week of August," recalls Adrian.

The players wore heavy old style sweatshirts and pants, not the best attire for vigorous exercise in the 95-degree summer heat.

"We had scrimmage every day, every day, every day. We would start around three in the afternoon and practiced until it was dark," says Adrian. "You just did jumping jacks or a little stretching or sit-ups, then you'd practice for two or three hours and then run wind sprints."

Coach Deville had a different wrinkle on practicing in the heat. He wouldn't allow the players to have any water!

Hunt says, "Coach Deville said if you don't drink during practice, you don't have to drink during the game. That was his philosophy and it worked. He worked us to no end."

As if dehydration and fatigue weren't enough, some of the players had to run home.

Norman Reed, left end on the championship team, recalls that jogging home was part of the workout.

"There wasn't anyone to come and pick us up; we didn't have cars. I lived about four miles out of town and many a day, jogging home was part of my workout," remembers Norman.

There were no weights or sophisticated fitness gear. The work at home on the farm served as weight training. Norman often had to milk a couple of cows and "get to the field with a shovel," even after a tortuous workout and a four-mile run.

Norman Reed also recalls that the helmets were heavy and hot, just adding to the discomfort of workouts. Despite these discomforts, or maybe because of them, Reed recalls these practices fondly.

"We had fun no matter what. We didn't know any better at the time. We did what we had to do," he recalls.

Coach Deville was not just a fan of dehydration, he also believed in pressuring talented athletes to join the team.

Adrian Hunt was initially the team manager.

"I didn't start playing until mid-season of my junior year, and the only reason I started playing was to get Coach off my tail," says Hunt.

In those days there were two free periods a day and all the football players from eighth grade up would get both of their free periods the last two hours before noon so they could get an extra practice in.

If the coach was a hard taskmaster and a persuasive pursuer of talent, he could also get his point across. Hunt recalls one such occasion.

"The funniest thing I remember was we had a young man who played end, and for some reason he couldn't remember his plays. On one of those hot days, he messed up one of the plays and Coach went ballistic.

"Coach ran up to him and said, 'Son, do you know your name?'

"He replied, 'Yes, sir.'

'Do you know where you live?'

He said. "Well, yes, sir I do."

"And at that, Coach Deville threw his hat on the ground, flipped forward onto his hands and kicked his feet straight in the air like a mule, screaming the whole time!"

Practice and repetition were programmed into the players, even if they didn't realize it.

Drop kicking was popular in six-man because a successful drop kick was worth two point. Adrian Hunt refined the art of drop-kicking and became the team's kicker.

"I lived in town, so I had to walk four or five blocks to school and the streets were all gravel. Allan Venable, the quarterback, and I lived by each other, so we walked to school together. We always had a handful of rocks, and we were either throwing them or dropping them and kicking them as they touched the ground. At the time we didn't actually know what we were doing, but we were actually learning how to drop kick," remembers Adrian.

Allan Venable was quite an athlete. Norman Reed recalls how the quarterback spared his blushes in the championship game.

"We had a play where the two backs would cross and the quarterback would fake to them and then give the ball to the left or right end. In this particular game, I was right end and I was wide open. There was nothing between me and the cotton patch behind the field. I felt sure I was going to score and I was carrying the ball like a loaf of bread. Suddenly, this guy came out of nowhere and stole the ball right out from my arm."

"The only guy who could stop him from scoring was Allan Venable and he caught up with him and tackled him. We stopped them from scoring on that possession but I got a pretty good chewing out for carrying the ball that way," says Norman.

Adrian Hunt is very complimentary about his friend and quarterback, Allan Venable.

"Allan could play for anyone, anywhere, even to this day. He could throw the football and he was great at faking, which was critical because the game was so fast you had to do something and he was good at faking. He was the heart and soul of our football team," says Adrian.

He also gave his friend another great compliment.

"He could throw a strawberry through a locomotive."

And that was before strawberries were genetically modified.

When Coach Deville wasn't directing practice or pretending to be a mule, he drew up quite a playbook. Because six-man football was so wide open, almost every play was designed to score a touchdown.

"We had quite a few plays. We didn't have a book, we had sheets of paper. Coach would draw them up on the blackboard and we then go practice them," says Adrian Hunt.

Inevitably, there were some trick plays, but they had to be reported to the referees before the snap.

Adrian Hunt recalls, "We had a guy called Valgene Cart who was playing center. Everyone called him Choker. I don't know how he got that name but the only person who ever called him by his real name was his mother. He was a sophomore but he was big, probably weighed 230 pounds."

And this was before foods were genetically modified.

"We had this one play where Choker would snap the ball to the quarterback and the quarterback would hand it right back to him. He would never get out of his crouch. The rest of us would all go our different ways and spread the defense and the next thing you knew Choker had the ball and was heading down the field," says Hunt.

The season started with a 20-8 victory over Bell City. Then came the decisive game, the one that determines a season and defines a team's destiny. Adrian Hunt explains.

"We were playing Creole and we were behind at halftime 44-6. They were throwing the ball over me like raindrops. All they had to do was catch it. At halftime, our coach did the smartest thing he did all year, he took me out and put Norman in my place on defense. Norman shut them down the rest of the way, and we ended up winning 46-44."

Shutting a team of Creole's quality out for an entire half was a remarkable achievement. It showed the team's character and gave them a huge shot of self-belief.

The team surged after that, winning their next eight games by an average of more than 36 points a game.

Having wrapped up a play-off spot, the team made the long trek to China for their next game. That's China, Texas, who were champions of their district. Inter-state games were rare, largely because of the cost and time of travel.

Orville Bobbitt recalls, 'The trip to Texas was the only time we got to ride on a greyhound bus and we thought that was impressive."

The rest of the schedule, designed to be against local opponents, wasn't so arduous.

'Typically, we just drove in cars to the games," says Bobbitt.

Adrian Hunt recalls the trip to China. This was before the days of interstate and well paved roads.

"We got on that bus and drove and drove and drove and finally we got to Beaumont. We stopped in Beaumont and watched a movie and then resumed our journey to China."

The Chinese were very hospitable hosts. After they had been beaten 42-12, they hosted a barbecue with everything the boys could want to eat and drink, which they did before getting on the bus for the long trek home.

"They were the finest people," recalls Hunt.

Getting off the bus proved hazardous on one occasion.

Hunt recalls, "We stopped some place to get a hamburger and everybody unloaded the bus. We were across the street from the restaurant and a guy named Gerald Raspberry was last off. He tried to catch up with us and ran around the front of the bus. There was an automobile coming the other way and it hit him head on. Luckily they were going slow. Gerald got up, dusted himself off and laughed about it all the way into the restaurant. All during the meal he was laughing about getting run over! Then he went out and played the entire game!"

I guess that's the way to take a hit.

The next game was the playoff against old rival Creole who had built a huge lead against Iota in their first meeting in that game of destiny. This time Iota didn't need to dig themselves out of a hole and won very comfortably 46-12. It meant that over three consecutive halves of play, Iota had outscored Creole 86-12.

Now it was on to the championship game.

The team's unbelievable run had really united the town and everyone came out to watch the games.

Hunt recalls, "We had a set of bleachers around the field. On the home side, it would probably hold 2000, maybe 2500 people, and those bleachers would be full. People would be standing around the field and parked in the streets watching. It really united the community."

The championship game was played in Lockport against Holy Savior. It was a tight game but Iota prevailed in a relatively low scoring game, 28-14. They had won the championship and completed an unbeaten season.

The season helped unite the town and ignite a pride and passion about football. The next season Iota switched to eleven-man football and found success. One member of the team, Gerald Frey went on to play for LSU and was part of their famous 1959 championship team.

The switch to eleven-man inevitably clouded the memory about that last six-man team's great achievement. In fact, the trophy was lost for a while, but a new principal, Dr. Gibson Miller, searched for it and found it back in a closet. The trophy and the memories were restored and now they are fully part of one small town's incredible sporting achievement – and history.

Team members:
Norman Reed, Ronald Reed, Adrian Hunt, Allan Venable, George Leger, Purvis Clement, Billy Steen, Herman LeJeune, Gaston Doucet, Valgean Cart, Joseph Lantz, James Lantz, Ronald Henderson, Norman Fruge, Gerald Frey, Orville Bobbit, Anthony Singleton, Ronnie Martin and Herby Miller.

Bottom, from left to right: George Leger, Adrian Hunt, Rurvis Clement, Billy Steen, Herman LeJeune, Norman Reed, Gaston Doucet, James Lantz, Allan Venable. Top: Valgean Cart, Joseph Lantz, Ronald Henderson, Norman Fruge, Gerald Frey, Ronald Reed, Orville Bobbett, Anthony Singleton, Ronnie Martin, Kirby Miller.

The "Lost Trophy" of Iota

# LSU Uniforms, a Dance, and a Brawl

## Denham Springs Yellow Jackets

Denham Springs was like many of the other schools mentioned in this book. In the 1940s it was a rural town with a small student body and not a lot to do on weekends. So when six-man football started in 1946 season there was something to unite the community, something to get passionate about. And sometimes those passions boiled over when it came to games against local rivals.

Denham Springs saw development in the early twentieth century in part because of the Springs waters apparent healing properties. It officially became a village in 1903, Governor Huey Long designated it a town in 1929 and Governor Lethar Frazier proclaimed it a city in 1957. If the Springs waters were heralded it was a different type of water that features in the sporting lore of the town.

However, let's back up. Six-man football came to Denham Springs in 1944. The 1946 Yellow Jackets had a surprising amount of talent for a small school, starting at the quarterback spot.

Jim Delaune, a scrawny 135-pounder, played quarterback for four years, the first two of which were six-man. Despite his small stature, however, DeLaune was no pushover.

He recalls how one day he took pity on some of the kids riding the bus who didn't have any school lunches. So he shared some of his peanut butter and jelly sandwiches with them.

"Then every day, they decided that they wanted part of my lunch. I had to tell them I wasn't giving them any more lunch, they had to get their own lunch somewhere. One of the older boys said he was going to bring his knife to school and I would have to give him my lunch. I said, 'No, I'm not going to give you lunch – I've got a knife, too."

Mr. Grady Hornsby was the principal and also the head coach. He had some assistance. Delaune recalls the coaching set-up.

"Our high school principal was our coach but he had a Methodist minister who sometimes would come out – I guess he played football somewhere. Nate Crawford who played eleven-man for Kansas State, came as an assistant coach," recalls Delaune.

Being the Principal, Hornsby was concerned about every aspect of the players' welfare.

"Mr. Hornsby was the Head Coach and he made sure that we were in condition and our discipline in school was good. He checked our grades and made sure we were all okay," says Delaune.

Leslie McDowell, a standout on those early teams, also recalls Hornsby's insistence on discipline.

"Mr. Hornsby put us through drills that really provided things for us in life. You take care of your buddy and your buddy takes care of you. This taught me many things that I used later in my life," recalls McDowell.

"Mr. Hornsby was definitely opposed to anyone smoking a cigarette or if you took a can of beer and if they knew about it, you were off the team. He didn't want you to have a date. He did not want you to have cokes. You couldn't have cold drinks," says McDowell.

Of course, the boys didn't always want to follow these rules.

"We used to leave practice and go to Power's Drugstore to get us a coke. Here comes Mr. Hornsby because the Post Office is next door. So he'd come from the Post Office and catch us all, and he'd run us the next day if he had caught us with a drink of coke. Discipline was the name of the game then," recalls McDowell.

The strict regimentation extended beyond the practice field.

"At Denham Springs school there was a boy's side and a girl's side and you didn't dare cross over to the girl's side if you were a boy. If you crossed that imaginary line there was no question, you just were taken right to the Principal's office and you got punished," says McDowell.

McDowell didn't regret the lessons learned on and off the sports field.

"Everyone I knew who was an athlete really took to the discipline and as a result came out better in life. They enjoyed life a lot more. They appreciated life and they knew what work was like. When my kids started playing ball in high school, I knew to leave them alone because the coach's discipline could do a lot more for them than I could."

McDowell was a long-legged basketball star, too. His friend, the quarterback Delaune, commented, "Leslie McDowell's legs were so long, you couldn't tackle a guy with legs as long as that."

Later, when he joined the Army, McDowell tried out for the basketball team.

"I went out for basketball and made the team there and we were runners-up in the all-Army tournament. Then, the next year I was shipped overseas and was in Germany. So, again I went out for basketball and I was selected for the team, and we played all of Europe, the European championships, and we won the European championship. That was in 1954."

After he came out of the Army and graduated, McDowell had a small job and one day got a surprise call.

"I got a call from Mr. Hornsby. He said he needed a basketball coach, and asked if I would be interested. The coach that he had hired had gotten sick and that's why he needed to have a coach at the last minute. I thought that sounds like fun. So, I came up to Denham Springs and took over the basketball team."

As you might expect, Hornsby the coach didn't cut the students any slack when they started practice in the July heat.

The school year began in July. The school year ended in April so that students could help with strawberry picking, after all this is strawberry country. After the strawberries, there were vegetables to pick and after that cotton.

So football practice started in the July heat.

"It was some hot, too. You get out there and you didn't dare drink water. You could drink water before the practice and a little bit after practice. And they gave you the salt tablets and, Lord, it was rough," remembers Delaune.

Leslie McDowell also recalls that there were other participants at practice.

"We had a lot of citizens in town that would like to come up and watch practice and even participate. This was right after the war. A lot of those returning veterans were coming back to high school and college," he remembers.

The lack of adequate gear or uniforms also posed another problem. Coach Hornsby came up with an idea.

Jim Delaune recalls.

"We didn't have any money to buy helmets or equipment so Mr. Hornsby sent me and Gordon Thompson over to LSU to talk to coaches and see if we could get some equipment. We weren't really able to get any, but we were in the dressing room with the players. In those days Zollie Toth was the fullback. Y.A. Tittle was the quarterback and Charlie Pevey was the second string quarterback. I took his jersey because he would come out to Denham Springs and give me a few pointers on how to be a quarterback."

Although the boys weren't successful in securing equipment for the team they had inventive ways of finding some for themselves.

Jim Delaune explains.

"My buddy who went with me to LSU decided he would take some thigh pads out of the locker room. I said 'Gordon what are you going to do? 'I'm going to put them under my pants and wear them out.' He said. 'No, you can't do that!.' I said. Zollie Toth was the fullback and he was down in the hallway talking to someone. And I said, 'How are you going to get past Zollie?'"

Gordon replied, "Well, you go down there and talk to him and I'm going to slip out behind y'all and take them out."

And Gordon got himself a pair of shoes and some thigh pads and got out.

"We would have been in a lot of trouble I suppose if he had been caught with them but he got a pair of shoes that fit him and thigh pads and that's all we got that day," recalls the former quarterback.

Leslie McDowell recalls the day some uniforms were officially delivered to the school.

"We started right after the war so we had no uniforms, no nothing. I remember seeing a truck drive up to school and two guys got out and started unloading it. What in the world is that? It was full of Southeastern uniforms that they had given to us. We wore them year after year. There was no replacing them. So not only were they hot, they were heavy, full of salt and everything because they had probably never been washed."

Preparation wasn't confined to the practice field. The players would go watch their rivals play frequently.

"Dutchtown and Gonzales played on Sunday afternoons and we played Friday nights. So, they would come over and watch us on Friday night and we'd go there on Sunday afternoon. Sometimes we traveled a pretty good distance just to see our opponents play. I know we went to Ville Platte a few times to watch them play," says Delaune.

Sometimes traveling to watch rivals play could be treacherous in itself.

"In those days there was no bridge across the Atchafalya basin all way across, so the water would come up sometimes, and we'd go through the water about knee deep to get to Ville Platte," says Delaune.

When they got to Ville Platte some unusual sights and sounds awaited them.

"In Ville Platte some of the people would come to the game in their horse and buggies," says Delaune. And when they played their rivals form across the Atchafalya basin there was another surprise.

Ville Platte called all their plays in French.

Une, deux, trois…hut, hut.

"We were the only football team in the parish so if you had any interest in football you'd come to Denham Springs. We had a big crowd watching us all the time. Our opponents were Gonzales, Dutchtown, St. Amant and St. Gabriel. We played Frankinton , too," says the once scrawny quarterback.

But Gonzales and especially Dutchtown, were the key rivals because the communities were intertwined.

Delaune recalls, "They combined the school at Prairieville and moved it to Dutchtown. I can remember those days because there was a big fight, turned over trucks and everything, because they didn't want to go to Dutchtown."

Moreover, some families had children who were enrolled, or had attended, both schools.

"Dutchtown was definitely our real rival and I think it was because my brothers had played football there. I played in Denham Springs and my dad was a deputy sheriff in Ascension Parish. When we moved to Denham Springs the rivalry was really tremendous," says DeLaune.

"Dutchtown and Gonzales would have those dances on Saturday nights before the games and they expected everyone who had children in the school to be there. They expected the parents to be there. The parents danced right along with the students, and the students and little kids all danced. It was a time when we didn't have TVs and things for people to do at home. So if you did anything, you were at the dance. I think the teachers gave us grades on whether we attended or not, but they certainly expected you to be there."

There was one incredible game against Dutchtown played in December 1946 that lives long in the memory. In the memory of most but not all who were there.

Leslie McDowell is the one with some amnesia.

"We were playing Dutchtown and it rained and rained. There was water everywhere and mud on the field. I kicked off the game and made the first tackle and then lined up as defensive back and made another tackle, and I don't remember anything from that point on. I stayed out until halftime."

Eventually, McDowell got some medical attention.

"They had me in the schoolhouse. I didn't even know where I was. There was a doctor there and he said to me, "Well, I think you're alright but you're a little disoriented." I know I started and played the whole second half but don't remember much about it. There was no face guard and I got a knee to the head and I didn't know what happened for two hours," says McDowell.

But McDowell's probable concussion was simply the start of an amazing series of events.

Dutchtown scored late on to take a 12-6 lead but Denham Springs scored with the last play of the game to win 13-12.

Jim Delaune recalls it like this:

"It had rained real hard. Boy, I mean it rained hard. Water was everywhere. There was one boy on our team who could kick the ball about as far as anyone I have ever seen. His dad kind of instigated the fight after the game and we had a regular free-for-all. I thought a few of them were going to drown. A few of them from Livingston Parish loved to fight anyway so it didn't take much."

The closeness of the communities, the dramatic finish, the inevitable drinking and betting, all contributed to a combustible ending. The teams were taken into the schoolhouse and watched the fisticuffs in relative safety of the gym.

A.E. Sutton's memory of the 'Dutchtown brawl' was recorded in an interview he gave to the Denham Springs-Livingston Parish News in April 1990.

"About an hour before the game people started pouring in. They were drinking that giggle water pretty heavy."

People were lined up ten deep along each sideline and the estimated crowd ballooned to about a thousand. A big fight broke out behind the goalpost even as the teams were warming up.

After the game, as both teams were watching from the gym, Sutton observed the following.

"Two old men were out there and they were fisticuffin' it pretty good. Directly, one hit the other up side the jaw and his false teeth flew out. He held up his hands and the other quit slugging him. He reached down and got his false teeth. There was a drainage ditch near him and he rinsed his teeth off and went back to fisticuffing but it wasn't long before they were both played out."

Leslie McDowell had recovered some of his memory by then because he recalls the post-game fracas this way.

"We had our center Raymond Starnes who had gotten bit by one of the Dutchtown boys. Starnes told his father, "Dad that's the guy that bit me." And that started the fight. So they got up and started after each other. And there was a big slew behind the schoolhouse where there was two feet of water and they started pushing each other under the water."

The chaos and the conflict exploded around three priests visiting from Sacred Heart of Ville Platte. Although a priest had been influential in bringing football to Ville Platte, probably many others weren't familiar with the game or the intense rivalry on display. Bewildered and astonished by the mayhem and disorder, the priests knelt down on the field and prayed. They might have offered up a different Hail Mary that night.

The fighting continued long after the final whistle.

Delaune recalls, "It lasted a long time and I don't know how the law got it under control. My dad was the marshal in Denham Springs for a number of years, and he was the only law they had. There was no way you could stop all the fistfights that went on that night."

Not all games were that exciting or that close. In fact, a mercy rule was in effect.

The quarterback recalls an incident involving his friend McDowell.

"We were playing in Franklinton and I think in those days if you scored more than 56 points they called the game. And Leslie was going to score a touchdown and we all hollered at him to fall down so we could keep playing."

McDowell was a versatile athlete. Arnet Crawford was a local who had played ball in college and went to play for the Philadelphia Eagles. He taught McDowell how to kick.

"I remember one game when I was punting out of the end zone. I told my teammate, 'Y'all just keep them off me and I'll see what I can do.' Well I got hold of a good one and it came to a stop on their one yard line," says McDowell.

In the end, Ville Platte proved to be Denham's nemesis. The two teams played consecutive years for the six-man championship and both times Ville Platte prevailed.

Delaune recalls the rivalry and how it developed.

"We played Sacred Heart of Ville Platte for the state championship and we lost to them. The next year we went to eleven-man and we played Ville Platte in out first game and we won. We thought we were going to win the state championship."

McDowell the basketball player would love to see six-man football make a comeback.

"I think it's a game I would love to see comeback. I would like to go see those kinds of games because then you can see everything in the whole game. You can see both lines because there are only twelve men on the field. And now when you've got twenty-two men and they're all piled up, you don't know what's going on. It makes six-man football a more interesting game."

"I haven't touched another football since December 1947. That was the last game that I played. But that was the best time of my life, and it's the best kind of athletics for a small school," adds Leslie.

Delaune cherishes the lessons from his school football experience.

"A lot of our leading citizens are from that football team. I also think that helped me get elected Mayor of Denham Springs, which I was for twelve years. Also, having been in the Marine Corps helped. Once you've been in the Marine Corps you going to stick up for whoever's running that's been in the Marine Corps along with you."

In his two seasons of coaching, Hornsby had a record of 18 wins 4 losses and 1 tie. In 1947 the Yellow Jackets went undefeated through the regular season and beat Buras in the South Louisiana Regional Championship 26-18. But they lost the next week to Ville Platte 28-6.

The members of that 1947 team were: Bill Davis, Dickie Barnett, Larry warner, Lane Barnett, Bernard Gaudin, Lawton Graham, Jimmy Geautreaux, Dale Hatchell, Robert Murray, Glen Gaudin, Gordon Thompson, Lathan Sutton, A.E. Sutton, Leslie McDowell, Cecil Benton, D.W. Stingfield, and Jim Delaune.

# 1947-48 FOOTBALL TEAM
## Taken from the first annual ever printed at DSHS called the "Buzz"!

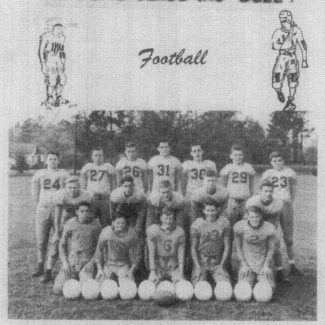

*Football*

| FRONT ROW: | SECOND ROW: | THIRD ROW: |
|---|---|---|
| Bill Davis | Lawton Graham * | Gordon Thompson * |
| Dickie Barnett | Jimmy Geautreaux * | Lathan Sutton * |
| Larry Warner | Dale Hatchell * | A. E. Sutton * |
| Lane Barnett * | Robert Murray * | Leslie Mc Dowell * |
| Bernard Gaudin | Glen Gaudin * | Cecil Benton * |
| | | D. W. Stringfield * |
| * Lettermen | | Jim De Laune * |

## 1947 Team

# 1945 DSHS Football Team

From bottom, left to right: Robert Boyor, Ned Benton, Hollis McAdams, Royce Wilson, Euel Jackson, Coach Bob Jamison, Carol Jordon, Milton Eisworth, Berlin Benton, Tommy Sullivan, Joe Causey, Hulon D. Miley

# A Napoleonic Mystery, Muscle, and the Coach's Wife Who Was Thrown Out of the Game

## Clinton Eagles

Clinton only played organized six-man football for one year but that year changed the lives of the many people involved. Not only did Clinton's six-man tradition cement lifelong relationships it was also an active witness to one of the most significant changes in sports physiology.

It's fitting that Clinton's six-man story is tenuously connected to a remarkable military commander. The town was itself the site of several encounters during the late unpleasantness sometimes referred to as the Civil War. Union general Benjamin Grierson occupied Clinton in June of 1863. The town was deserted as the Confederates had moved to the north. In 1864 Union General Lee also raided Clinton destroying a tannery along the way. In March 1865, a month before the end of the war between the states, Union general Francis Herron defeated a depleted Confederate force in the town.

More recently, movie directors have replaced union generals as interlopers in the picturesque town. *Dukes of Hazard, Sounder* and the classic *Long, Hot Summer* were all filmed in and around the town. HBO has currently a long-term contract with the town for its series *True Blood*.

There was, no doubt, plenty of blood in the long, hot summer that preceded the 1947 six-man football season. At the center of the action, as always, was the coach, in this case one Marshall Ney Williams.

"Mr. Rogers came to see him (Marshall) at our country store and asked him if he would like to start an athletic program at Clinton," recalls the coach's wife Alberta.

"His first day he got all the eligible boys who wanted to play football in the auditorium and decided it would need to be a six-man team," Alberta adds.

In fact, there were only three boys who had ever played organized football before and the average weight was about 135 pounds. That included Albert Moffit who was so oversized at nearly 400 pounds that two jerseys had to be stitched together as there wasn't one that fit him. Marshall Ney, the coach, had his work cut out for him.

According to the family, Marshall's grandfather liked Napoleon, the French emperor not the brandy. It's unclear how much the family actually knew about Marshall Ney, but he is one of the most enigmatic characters of the Napoleonic era and someone who, no doubt, would have made a great coach.

Ney, the French general, grew up in the Lorraine area of France, near the German border and in a region that was always a focus of conflict between the two countries.

Ney left a brief career as a civil servant and enlisted in the French army. He was soon commissioned and rose through the ranks becoming a cavalry general in 1796. In a cavalry charge against the Austrians during the French Revolutionary Wars, he was thrown from his horse and taken prisoner but was later exchanged for an Austrian general.

In May 1804, Ney was made Marshal of the Empire and given command of part of Napoleon's La Grande Armee. He fought bravely in numerous battles that raged in central Europe. He captured Innsbruck and successfully besieged Magdeburg. He arrived just in time to save Napoleon from defeat at Eylau in what has been described as "a tie". There was no overtime in the Napoleonic era.

He fought in Spain and Portugal and delayed Wellington long enough to give the French army time to retreat in 1811. He was then removed from command for insubordination but was reinstated and given command of the third corps of La Grande Armee during the invasion of Russia. He was wounded in the neck at Smolensk and later led the retreat from Russia. He led from the back, and was called the "last Frenchman on Russian soil," which prompted Napoleon to call him "the bravest of the brave".

He fought heroically and was wounded many times in numerous actions but led the Marshal's revolt, refusing to march on Paris and insisting Napoleon abdicate. The monarchy thus restored, were grateful and Louis XVIII made Ney a peer.

When Napoleon re-launched his campaign against the monarchy, Ney initially was determined to protect the king and vowed to bring Napoleon back alive in an iron cage. However, when he went to meet the former emperor he was persuaded to switch sides. He was made commander of the left wing of Napoleon's Army of the North.

He led a cavalry charge against British cannons at the decisive battle of Waterloo but ultimately failed, but not for want of effort. He had five horses killed from under him during the fighting.

With Napoleon's defeat, Ney was arrested in December 1815 and sentenced to death for treason. He apparently was given the privilege of giving the firing squad the orders for his death and was reported to have said: "Soldiers, when I give the command to fire, fire straight at my heart. Wait for the order. It will be my last to you. I protest against my condemnation. I have fought a hundred battles for France, and not one against her ... Soldiers, Fire!"

He was buried in Paris. Or was he?

Various theories suggest that Ney's execution was a fake, and he ran the ball all the way to the United States. One theory was that no less than the Duke of Wellington himself ran interference for him due to their mutual Masonic ties. Whatever the truth, the fact is that records indicate that a man calling himself Peter Stuart Ney did indeed arrive in Charleston, South Carolina, a few weeks after Ney's execution date. Records show that he was a schoolteacher in Brownsville, South Carolina before moving to North Carolina where he held jobs in Hillsborough, Salisbury and Third Creek. He spent some time in Virginia but returned to the Mocksville Third Creek area, where he died in 1846, aged 77. His gravestone has the inscription,

"A native of France and soldier of the French Revolution under Napoleon Bonaparte."

Forty years later, his grave was exhumed and a plaster cast of the skull made. It was subsequently lost then found and, according to informal analysis, showed evidence of "having been scarred by bullets and swords."

That's quite an act to follow but Clinton's Marshall Ney had some of the same qualities: charisma, leadership, and courage. Marshall Ney, the coach, was also a man of principle. After coaching he became the school principal and then was offered the superintendent's job.

His wife Alberta remembers when he was offered the job.

"He said he would take the job but he wanted to talk to John Harris first, because John had been in the system longer and he didn't want to jump ahead of him if Harris wanted the position. John didn't, but he came to work as the assistant superintendent."

The coach was characteristically fair and an inspiration to his players. He had a passion for football and for coaching.

Alberta says, "The one regret was that he had to leave his coaching career. He said he loved his boys. They respected him. They laughed with him. He said they tried everything they could to do what he was telling them and he thought the cooperation he got from the boys, their parents, the town, all the support he got, was what made life so good for him."

The coach led practices from the front. Toller Hatcher was a running back on the team and recalls long, hot practices with no water, as was the prevailing philosophy at the time.

"'For practice uniforms we had old shell pants left over from the group that played prior to us. They were white jerseys and cotton and hot as blazes. You made it a few laps around the field with one of those things on and in a few minutes they were soaking wet and they start out down to your waist but by the time you run three laps, the tail was down to your knees and soaking wet," he recalls.

Moreover, there was another hazard to contend with. "We practiced on the clay hill behind the school, red clay. If the red clay got in your clothes it never came out."

But soon practice was over and the season was about to begin. So on September 23rd, the Clinton boys put their reputations on the line in a home game against Mt. Hermon.

"My dearest friend Charles Wilson kicked off the first game and he was nervous. He was afraid he was going to miss the ball and he was scared to death. I said, 'Just kick the ball, Charles. It don't matter. It'll go somewhere.' And he did," recalls Hatcher.

A newspaper account of the game reported it like this.

"Receiving the kickoff, and trying unsuccessfully to gain three times, Mt. Hermon punted to the Eagles. Polk received the punt on his own 35-yard line and raced it back to the Mt Hermon 1-yard line."

Imagine that. The first touch of the ball by an Eagles player is a punt return to the opponent's one-yard line! On the next play, Polk drove though the line for a touchdown. The newspaper account continues.

"A few plays later the Eagles gained possession of the ball again, and Schmidt scored on the first play. White then executed the perfect drop kick for the two extra points. We kicked off and on Mt. Hermon's first play, White intercepted a pass and raced for a third touchdown."

Clinton won that first home game 34-0. Hatcher says it lifted the team.

"We had two or three pretty good players on our team. Sid White was our quarterback and Hubert Polk was the star running back. We just felt great about our first game and we didn't even dream we'd win a game. So we got off to a good start and it looked like we might have a successful year."

Hatcher remembers that, "I played on offense and defense, we all did. With six guys on the team you had to play both ways because there wasn't enough players. There were very few substitutes. If you went out of the game, you went back in pretty quick."

Ten days later, Clinton hosted Jackson and Hatcher's defensive play was decisive. It was scoreless with two minutes of the first half to go when Hatcher deflected an intended pass, Polk caught it and raced the length of the field for a touchdown. Clinton won 33-13.

Hatcher recalls, "That was one of the highlights of the season because Clinton didn't like Jackson and Jackson didn't like Clinton."

Hatcher recalls that in the next game against Napoleonville the Eagles got a dose of reality. "They were bigger and faster than us and we got taught a lesson in football."

The score line, however was respectable, a 26-14 loss.

The next week it was on the road at Mt. Hermon. The newspaper covered it this way.

—

"Mt. Hermon scored first but the Eagles quickly struck back. White's deadly passes went everywhere. Herrod received two of them for a touchdown and extra point. Wilson scored the second touchdown then Herrod opened the second period by recovering a fumble for a touchdown. Mt. Hermon then scored but on the kickoff White reversed to Polk who went all the way."

It turned into a rout with Clinton winning 51-20.

Hatcher was a 119-pound running back. After graduating he found himself in the Army stationed at Ft. Riley, Kansas.

"I was asked whether I would like to play football and I said, "no." I had seen a lot of Army guys and they were four times as big as me! So I became the person who took care of injuries, not just for the football team but for other sports, too, like boxing, basketball and baseball. We had some all-American athletes there."

"The boxing team won the championship one year and the battalion commander gave us all a three day pass. As far as I know one of those kids still ain't back. He went to Mexico and I don't think he ever returned."

Hatcher was later a trainer for the Clinton high school team under his former quarterback now coach, Sid White. He did the taping and wrapping for all the players and was at every game. "We beat everybody we played that year," he recalls of an eleven-man team.

Hatcher had a pretty good career at LSU. He went to work in their training department with Marty Broussard, who was well known and a trainer for the U.S. Olympic team. And this was at a time when training methods were on the cusp of change.

There were two training myths in this era. The first was the drinking water was bad for you. The second was that weightlifting impeded athletic development by making the boys too muscle bound.

Robert Hodges came to Clinton shortly after the school switched to eleven-man.

"I was never successful in my football endeavors but I played like everyone else. Because if you were male you were chicken if you weren't out there playing."

Hodges couldn't understand the ban on weight lifting.

"Weight lifting was bad for you and you could be kicked off the team for doing it because it would make you slow, muscle-bound and in general ruin your athletic ability. I didn't have any athletic ability anyway so that didn't scare me and I promoted it in the school, in the community, this outside activity of weight lifting and body building."

"There were people in Clinton who really took offense that I was promoting this sabotage among the school boys by getting them to lift weights. It was going to ruin their athletic ability they thought. In our yearbook there's a page that shows a number of us in a weightlifting meet, which I had organized, and it shows me completing a 100 pound press," says Rodgers.

"I went to the Alvin Roy Health studio in Baton Rouge, which was something revolutionary and new, and I worked out there some. I got some training from Alvin and then I organized a weightlifting competition in Clinton, and some of Alvin's people came to help put the project on and to judge."

Alvin Roy was an innovator. Born in Baton Rouge he played football and basketball for Istrouma High School. He went to LSU making the basketball team as a walk-on. He joined the Army in 1941 and later served under George Patton winning four battle stars as well as a bronze star. By 1946 he was organizing athletic events and was designated as an aide to the US weightlifting team which brought him into direct contact with the legendary coach Bob Hoffman and Roy saw first hand the value of weightlifting for athletic performance.

In 1947 Roy opened a health club and promoted weightlifting for health and athletic performance. He was the US Olympic weightlifting team trainer for the 1952 Helsinki Olympics in which the US won the gold medal.

Enter into the picture 'Big Fuzzy' and 'Little Fuzzy,' the Brown twins who were Alvin's old high school coach and principal. Initially, they declined Roy's attempts to introduce weightlifting into the football training regimen but he eventually persuaded them to give it a try. There was one notable holdout. Billy Cannon, who played football, basketball and ran track at the school, didn't want to jeopardize his speed and thus the chances of a college scholarship by making himself muscle-bound. But when Cannon saw the advances his teammates were making he decided to give weight training a try too.

By the time football season rolled around, the entire squad with the exception of one player, had made significant athletic gains. The Istrouma football team went undefeated, four players made all-state and Cannon scored a state record 229 points and averaged 10 yards a carry. The team also had fewer injuries than at any time in their history.

Cannon went off to LSU, who had a disappointing 5-5 record in his first season. Coach Dietzel was still skeptical about weight training but as with his high school coaches, Roy convinced the coach to incorporate weight training. Expected to finish ninth in the SEC, LSU went undefeated in the 1958 season, winning its first national championship and making Dietzel Coach of the Year. And so the notion that weightlifting was bad for athletes was finally debunked.

Robert Hodges feels he had some small part to play in exploding the myth about weightlifting.

"It was fun for me to be an upstart, have my own group and promote what I believed in and to see that it became the prevailing view in athletics in general and in college football," he says.

"Deese Powers was the most successful body builder in Clinton. He was not very good in his studies and so he was sent to Georgia Military Academy and he did great under that kind of discipline. While he was there, based on the work-outs we had been doing in Clinton, usually in his barn, he won the Academy's physique contest. He had gone from a beanpole to the most outstanding bodybuilder in that big military school," says Hodges proudly.

On Halloween, the Eagles had to face plenty of tricks, which was no treat when they were scheduled to play a tough and bigger Denham Springs team. A rainstorm was so severe that it actually halted the game for a while and also slowed up Clinton's speedy players. But Denham Springs' overall quality finally told in a 51-18 victory although the Eagles did have three touchdowns called back.

At that game was cheerleader, Gay Marie Benekey McKutchen.

"I was elected to be one of the cheerleaders when Clinton started six-man. I was so excited because I just really loved going to Clinton High. To me, any school day was a really good day. I lived out in the country where there were no close folks for me to have any friends," she recalls.

She may have loved being at the games but her guardians were not that thrilled. Gay was raised by her aunt and uncle. Her uncle was severely disabled with rheumatoid arthritis and her aunt was allergic to milk. Which left Gay as the only available person to perform an important twice daily routine.

"I was literally the milk maid at my house. Every morning before school and every afternoon after school, I milked a cow. I think that's why they weren't thrilled about my cheerleading – it took me away from my milking duties," Gay says.

Gay says that one of the great parts of being a cheerleader was meeting the cheerleaders of the other teams. "I remember at half-time we would go across the field and introduce ourselves and get to know each other," she recalls.

Don Howard, Eddie Clemmens, Voncile Howard, Pat Bowles, Betty Jean McKay and Gay Marie Boeneke were the other cheerleaders.

The cheerleaders were back in action the following week when Clinton played Jackson.

The newspaper reported the early action like this.

"Within a minute of play, Polk had sprinted forty yards for our first touchdown. White drop kicked the extra points. Jackson scored towards the last of the first period, but White reversed to Polk on the kickoff and again Polk went all the way. During the second period Herrod scored on a double reverse. White was again successful kicking the extra points." Clinton won 30-14.

Weather delayed the rematch with Denham Springs by five days but that wasn't enough time for three key Eagles to recover from injuries and Denham Springs won 39-6. In the next game Toller Hatcher intercepted a pass and ran it 45 yards back for a touchdown and Polk passed for two more on the way to 20-7 win against Mt. Hermon.

Going into their final game at Jackson Clinton had a 5-3 record. Jackson got out to an early 13-0 lead but the Eagles came back to tie. With less than four minutes to go Jackson took the lead. The Eagles then drove down the field but with second down and goal on the four-yard line, time expired.

The team had captured the imagination of the town and enhanced community spirit.

"I don't remember how many people were at the games but the people of Clinton have always been very supportive of any athletic event, particularly football. After the first game the fans were very happy. We had football back in Clinton. And we were tickled to death to be playing and pleasing the folks of Clinton," Toller Hatcher remembers.

This community enthusiasm and esprit de corps was evident some twenty years later when Marshall Ney Williams the coach turned superintendent, and his wife went to cheer the Eagles on in a big road game.

Alberta Williams takes up the story.

"The boys were playing their hearts out and they were winning. I was nervously watching the clock. I was one of our loudest cheerleaders. I could have even led the real ones on the field. I watched the clock and I thought the game was over. So, of course, I left the stand and ran out into the middle of the field, hugging the boys, telling them what a wonderful game they played and how proud I was of them," Alberta says.

Then something went horribly wrong.

"Then all of a sudden there was a whistle. Everything stopped. The referee walked up to me and took me by the arm and said, 'Lady this game is not over. When you get off the field we will resume.'"

It was the rarely seen 'illegal woman downfield' call.

"I had to turn around and face all my friends sitting and watching and now laughing their heads off. It was funny to them but I was really embarrassed."

But this embarrassment went into overtime.

"So, the game finally ended and we were on our way home. My husband said, 'Let's stop at this little restaurant.' It was Laplace and as we came through the door there were the three referees sitting at a table eating. And one of them said to the others in a loud voice that everyone in the restaurant could hear, 'There's that lady that I had to throw off the field tonight.'"

But for Alberta, football was her family and her family was football.

"One of the best things that I can remember is how much football was played in our family. We have three boys all of whom played. My daughter was a cheerleader. We met so many people. We had contact with so many schools. There were many, many schools who tried to get my husband to transfer to their school system and to coach for them. He was always appreciative of their wanting him but his heart was in Clinton," Alberta says.

Alberta has a favorite story that reflects the fact that football is embedded in almost every family tradition and memory.

"My husband wanted to go scouting talent at a local game about the time our youngest child was due," says Alberta.

Marshall asked his wife whether she was sure it was okay for him to go.

"I said, yeah, go ahead. I've had these babies before and I think I know when he's coming or not," said Alberta.

Marshall duly left with a couple of buddies and headed to the game. He was watching the game when an announcement came over the loudspeaker asking for him. He knew what the message was before he was out of his seat. He raced to the hospital at Centreville.

"Of course, I got there ahead of him," recalls Alberta. "My sister and brother-in-law lived right next door and they took me. Well, by the time Marshall got to the hospital the baby was born. The doctor asked me 'what are we going to name this boy?'"

Alberta thought for a minute and then replied.

"Call him Football."

The doctor looked at Football's mom quizzically.

"That was what my husband has been doing all these married years and I had gotten so accustomed to football, that's the first thing I thought of," remembers Alberta.

Alberta reflects on her life.

"The people here have been good to us. We have friends. I have friends now. My husband has been gone several years and I still have friends and the boys who played for him are like my children. As I am now living alone, I help my granddaughter in her business. She moved her deli to Clinton after we lost our country store to fire in November 2011. It's great at the deli as we see people that come in who have been longtime friends. We hug each other. It's like brother and sister meeting again and I can't say thanks enough to Clinton and the boys who played, the families that were involved, how much they really mean to me and my family."

Albert Moffit & John Hatcher, 1947

Coach Marshall Vey Williams

# An Inspiring Priest, Some Vegetables, and a Civic Tradition

## Sacred Heart of Ville Platte Trojans

In any small town, one person can make a big difference. And if that person has passion, charisma and God on his side, the impact can be enormous. Throw in a few vegetables, a coach whose record as a civics teacher is unsurpassed and you have a recipe for an amazing story.

Ville Platte was founded by Marcellin Garand, an adjutant major in the Napoleonic army. The French tradition is evident everywhere in Ville Platte with many people speaking Francais. The Creole and Cajun influences are also omnipresent. Though a relatively small town with an approximate area of a little more than 3 square miles and a current population of about 8000, Ville Platte is home to Louisiana's largest state park. Chicot state park covers 6400 acres and is visited by thousands of people from all over the country and beyond each year.

The Sacred Heart Catholic School was started in Ville Platte in 1913 and operated by the Sisters of Carmel, an order of Canadian nuns. It was forced to close in 1928 because of the extreme economic conditions of the time. However, Father Maurice Bourgeois arrived in 1930 and a year later was able to re-open the school. One hundred children in grades one through five were taught by a different order of Canadian nuns, the Sisters of Our Lady of the Sacred Heart from New Brunswick. In 1935 grades 6 through 8 were added.

Father Irving DeBlanc arrived in the mid-thirties and became the first Associate Pastor of Sacred Heart Church. He instituted extra-curricular activities at the school, specifically football, basketball, boxing, band and elocution. In 1940 the school held its first high school graduation for fourteen students. New facilities including classrooms and a gym were completed in 1949 using army surplus buildings and substantial donations. The actual cost of $90,000 was about a third of the initial estimate.

Father DeBlanc traveled the area, recruiting children for the Catholic school, which wasn't easy because the school was not free, there was no transportation and DeBlanc emphasized the full involvement of both students and their parents. However, Father DeBlanc was a very charismatic and passionate man who was to have a huge influence on the town. He caught the imagination and was an incredible leader and motivator. He also started the town's first library.

DeBlanc's emphasis on sports led to the six-man football team, which played one of its first games in 1935. The local *Gazette* newspaper reported on the school's surprising win against a local team.

"In one of the most surprising upsets of the football year, a team from Sacred Heart Convent humbled the overconfident Ville Platte High School Cyclones 12-6 before a large assembly of fans who witnessed this struggle of titans on the gridiron here Sunday afternoon."

Raoul "Cow" Landry had volunteered to coach, and Tom Hewitt and Jack Reed were assistants.

While the team continued to be in formation, Fr. DeBlanc, officially became the First Assistant to Father Bourgeois, who had spent years trying to raise funds for amongst other things, a new church. Father Bourgeois instituted a new system of church finance. A voluntary admission charge of 10c for an adult and 5c for a child replaced the pew rental scheme.

In keeping with DeBlanc's ethos of pushing oneself to the limit, Ville Platte's first game in 1938 was played against New Iberia, who were state champions. The Trojans played a great game and held their illustrious opponents to an 8-8 tie. The following week they won 23-0 over Rayne Wolves. They lost a rematch against New Iberia but beat everyone else that year to finish with a 9-1-1 record.

Judge John Saunders of the Court of Appeal recalls the early days.

"Six-man football began when Monsignor DeBlanc, then Father DeBlanc, came to Ville Platte and initiated extra-curricular activities including football. He recruited coach Landry, who was a wonderful coach and Fr. DeBlanc went around town recruiting players. The first ones that come to mind were the Vegetable Boys."

The vegetable boys? They were the three Fontenot brothers. They apparently got their nicknames because of their interest in a neighbor's vegetable garden. Harold was named after a cucumber, Russell after a cabbage, and Lawrence after the eggplant. Another brother, Willis, wasn't a member of the vegetable family but did play football, possibly as a corn-erback. Apparently the boys were aggressive, had plenty of energy and were in frequent fights.

Despite their quirky monikers, the Fontenots were great athletes and were a backbone of the early team. In fact, two of the boys, Harold and Lawrence were co-captains of that first 1938 team. Their outstanding first competitive season would have got Ville Platte into the playoffs, but none existed at the time.

Between the 1938 and 1939 seasons there was plenty of discussion about a playoff system, and after further review, one was instituted. Father DeBlanc was the Secretary-Treasurer of the newly formed six-man conference.

In the following 1939 season Sacred Heart beat St. Martinville 20-6, in their first game then ran the board, outscoring their opponents 350-92. This took them into the newly formed southeast Louisiana championship game on December 1 at New Iberia stadium.

An enthralling game was played before a packed house. The Trojans used their vegetable connection to open the scoring with Lawrence lateralling the ball to brother Harold who raced in for the score. The Panthers drove to the Trojan one yard line with time about to expire in the first half. The ball was fumbled and Trojan end Leroy Soileau picked up the ball and headed full speed 78 yards in the other direction. Pat Vidrine, New Iberia's best athlete, tried to chase him down and caught him just before the goal-line as time expired. In the second half a Harold Fontenot pass to Guillame Guillory was enough to seal a victory despite Vidrine's score for New Iberia. The final was 20-6.

Sacred Heart then played northern Louisiana champions Greenwood with Greenwood prevailing 24-18 by virtue of their extra points efficiency. In two seasons Ville Platte had a record of 20-2-1.

The following year, Sacred Heart once again had a strong team.

Judge John Saunders recalls. "In 1941, the Kildare team had been Texas state champions. There were a powerhouse team and six-man was big in Texas. Coach Landry wanted his team to play the best of the best. He invited Kildare to come to play Sacred Heart. It was a match of titans but the Trojans beat Kildare 26-15."

The Trojans won their first three league games by a combined score of 128-0 and then took on a strong Menard team at home, and won 27-20. They were about to run the table again until they played St. Martinsville on the road.

The Sacred Heart travelling fans chanted "we were robbed" after St. Martinsville won the game. Sour grapes perhaps? The blinkered perception of passionate fans? Well, perhaps not, when you consider that Sacred Heart amassed more than six hundred yards of penalties and had five touchdowns called back!

That's unnecessary refness.

Jimmy Fruge, who tried out for the 1938 team at the age of 12 and ultimately played for three seasons, recalled the scene after the game.

"Bram (Lawrence Fontenot) said to the referee 'You robbed us.' The ref replied, 'We sure did. You robbed us last year in Ville Platte, this was payback.' That's when the fight began. We were badly outnumbered and might have been hurt but Father DeBlanc raised his arms and asked for peace. Suddenly, the warring factions parted and peace was restored."

Bob Soileau a young student at the time but later standout athlete and then coach at the school, recalls that the players tended to be small, fast, and tricky.

"We were not big, maybe 140 to165 pounds. But we had speed and coach Landry was a sprinter himself. Not just in high school and college but I think he went to the Olympics in the 440 yard dash but pulled a muscle and couldn't finish. He was also the king of reverses. He had plays where he would hand the ball off three times in the backfield before they crossed the line of scrimmage and sometimes he'd have the quarterback fake to everybody and just walk around like he has nothing to do with the ballgame and then throw a touchdown pass."

Judge John Saunders is also complimentary about the coach.

"Coach Landry was an exceptional coach. He got them in shape by running, he showed them how to play well, he inspired them more than he intimidated them and he made them believe in themselves. So you had a good coach, a good system and good community involvement."

The coach was a stickler for repetition.

Leroy Soileau recalls that, "We'd run the same play maybe ten or twelve times. He would repeat things all the time. He was a very intelligent coach because he'd make the offensive line and backs do the same thing, time and time again. Rayford Leblanc came in as coach in my senior year. He cared for the players and he worked hard. Let's do it until we do it right and once you do it right then you become a champion."

During the war years, gas rationing made travel difficult. Coach Landry realized that they wouldn't be able to travel far or often. In 1942 he reworked the schedule and travel arrangements to ensure the full schedule was played, which meant playing four games in nine days.

They won them all.

Lionel Pitre was a triple threat as he ran, passed and kicked. The Judge describes him as "perhaps the fastest player of his time". Lionel was the state champion in the 100 yard and 440 yard dash with times of 10.1 and 53 seconds respectively.

On playing games four in nine days, Pitre said, "That was fine. We were in shape. We practiced as hard as we played. We had lots of players. We would have played everyday if they would have let us."

Coach Landry would work the boys but wouldn't abuse them and he didn't overwork them. He focused on skill sets, co-ordination, and co-operation.

Those four wins in nine days set up a home game against Hanson Memorial of Franklin, the team to beat in the division. Melvin Tate had three touchdowns, Russell Fontenot scored a crucial fourth touchdown and Pitre kicked well to give the Trojans a 26-12 win. This took Ville Platte into the southern regional playoff against Jeanerette. However, because of war-related cancellations, the game ended up being for the state championship – and it was to be played in Ville Platte. The score was tied 20-20 at the end of three quarters but Jeanerette scored the final touchdown for a 28-20 victory.

There have been some outstanding athletes both for Sacred Heart and elsewhere in the league.

Bobby Soileau, the kid and later the coach, remembers that Sonny Stevenson was a great athlete. He won a couple of state championships as a heavyweight and he played quarterback on the six-man team. "He was a great passer and a pretty doggone good runner. Brother Bobby was a big boy who played quarterback also," says Bobby.

Judge Saunders agrees. "Sonny may just have been the best athlete to come out of Ville Platte. He played center his first year and second year. He went to quarterback when they went to eleven-man."

"Conrad Audoin was a good friend of Sonny's and also played on the line. When they'd get into a tough game they'd move Sonny and Conrad into the backfield. They were big strong fellows and nobody could tackle them. They were leaders even if they were young players. They were two of the better football players to come out of this town."

Judge Saunders recalls how Sonny and Conrad fared in the military.

"Both Sonny and Conrad were in the military because the war was on and they played military football for some outstanding teams. Sonny was on a base that had a very large contingent and a very top football team. He went out for the team and they said just about everybody on the team had played college ball but after they let him carry the ball a couple of times they decided they needed him on the team. He played quarterback and running back and they were so good they even played exhibition games against the L.A. Rams and the San Francisco 49ers. Sonny had to play defense against "Crazy Legs" Hirsch and he said that was like trying to cover Bobby Soileau."

The judge recalls another great player in the league.

"Charlie Cloud Jr. moved from Texas as a freshman and tried out for Mamou but they thought he was too small. But when they saw him running they figured no-one was going to catch him, so it didn't matter how big he was. He scored more points in six-man than anyone else in the state and he's reputed to have averaged 21 yards per carry."

It was 21 yards and the dust of Cloud.

Sacred Heart also had a legendary kicker called Wilbert Soileau.

Judge Saunders reminisces that, "Once they had a penalty on the extra point try, so they moved him back 15 yards. He's already 7 yards behind the line of scrimmage, 15 more makes 22, two more makes 24 and the goal post is 10 yards farther back – that's 34 yards. He drop kicked the extra point 34 yards. That's incredible"

Bobby Soileau remembers Wilbert practicing by kicking over the telephone lines. "He'd kick those things 35 feet in the air and at least 35 or 40 yards."

Bobby Soileau became coach in 1959 after a stellar intercollegiate career. He went to LSU after graduating from Sacred Heart. He weighed 126 but was twice the national boxing champion and won the Brink Trophy for the best boxer in the state of Louisiana. Bobby took Sacred Heart to the state eleven-man football championship in 1967.

Bob had some unconventional ways of firing his team up. In preparation for an upcoming championship game against Sicily Island he resorted to an unconventional move.

Bobby Dardeau, an assistant suggested, "I can get an airplane and I can have it fly over and drop some leaflets."

"I've got the leaflets ready made," said the coach.

After some deliberations they decided that the day before the game would be the best time to drop the leaflets and fire up the players. At the duly appointed time, coach asked the principal to allow the students to go outside. Bemused, the principal agreed.

Soon, a plane buzzed overhead and leaflets fell from the sky. They said, "SAVE THE TRIP -- WE HAVE STATE!"

When he wasn't coaching or organizing propaganda drops, Soileau taught a civics class. He must have been some teacher! His 1959 class produced a record number of six candidates for public office. These candidates have run for office 24 times between them and been elected 18 times which makes that a great .750 winning percentage.

The 1946 and 1947 teams were built around incredible speed, which took them to consecutive championships. As mentioned, Bobby Soileau coached the 1967 eleven-man to the championship.

Coach and civics teacher Bob Soileau and Judge John Saunders agree that in their joint experience, athletes typically don't get into trouble with the law.

Judge John Saunders speculates on that lack of association between crime and sports.

"It might be that the fellows who are disciplined are the fellows who have gone and played football, and it might be that the fellows who played football learn discipline. I do sit on the Court of Appeal and see an awful lot of things you wouldn't want to see. You just don't see fellows or ladies who played sports in high school, played ball, ran track, went into boxing, in trouble with the law. You don't see them unemployed or doing drugs. They basically learn how to play by the rules of society."

The 1938 team included Harold Fontenot, Lawrence Fontenot, Allen 'Goose" Fontenot, Leroy Soileau, Dale Fuselier, Herbet Fuselier, Guillame Guillory, Nathan Deville, Lionel Vidrine, Paul Ortego, Kirby Dupre, George Pitre, Norman Vidrine, Melvin Tate and Lionel Tate.

These guys were the nucleus of the teams that went on to post a record of 51 wins and four losses in the years 1938-1942. The Trojans completed their one decade of six-man football with both the 1936 and 1937 state championships. That's an achievement well worth remembering.

Father Irving A. DeBlanc

THE FIRST TROJAN FOOTBALL TEAM

Bottom, left to right: Harold Fontenot, Norman Vidrine, Van Ortego, Lionel Pitre, Marcialle Deville. Middle: Coach Landry, Nathan Vidrine, Vernon Lafleur, LeRoy Soileau, Gaumin Guillory, Kirby Dupre, Harold P. Fontenot, Father DeBlanc. Top: Alvin Tate, Jimmie Fruge, Sherman Fontenot, Melvin Tate, Russell Fontento, Herbert Fontenot.

# The Levee, Cardboard Helmets and a Converted Dad

## Brusly Panthers

Walt Lemoin has been the Principal of Brusly High school for twenty-five years. In the fall of 2013, on the hundredth anniversary of the school, he had a reunion that included many of the school's athletic greats as well as distinguished graduates and thirty-three homecoming queens. Among the attendees, was former mayor Rod Prejean a long time voice of Panther football, and Rod's son, the current commentator. There was plenty to talk about and remember.

Brusly has an area of about two square miles and a current population of about two thousand people. It is situated on the west side of the Mississippi in West Baton Rouge Parish. It was originally called Brusly Landing as it was a place where cargo ships stopped on the busy river. Brusly played six-man football between 1949 and 1962 and played in the 1958 championship game. Its proximity to the river gave it a characteristic feature – a levee.

The levee proved to be the focal point of training, discipline and practice.

Donald Morales, who played halfback and defensive back from 1959 to 1962, recalls the impact of training on the levee.

"A lot of practices were on the levee, going up and down. The offense was going down the levee and the defense was going up. It strengthened my legs and the ability to play ball," Morales says.

The levee wasn't just used for practicing plays it was also used for physical conditioning.

"At the end of practice we had to carry the biggest guy on the team up and down the levee. There was no conditioning other than carrying a man," recalls Morales.

L.J. Dupuy, a star quarterback, running back and punter in the 1958 to 1961 seasons, also remembers the levee practices.

"We practiced out on the levee and if you haven't had the opportunity to hit a man coming down that levee head on, then you haven't played Brusly six-man football. You weren't afraid of anyone on the ball field after that. Every team that played us knew we were going to hit hard and that's because of the time we spent practicing on the levee," says Dupuy.

The rationale of playing defense uphill is that you learned to get in the right position and stay low to make the tackle.

"All you had to do was hit a runner above the waist went he is running down the levee and you would learn why you need to stay low when tackling," says Dupuy.

Dupuy's father, originally against his son playing football, eventually relented and tried to help with strength training by making some improvised weights. He poured concrete in different size buckets and put a pipe between the buckets making a form of improvised weights. Many of the Brusly players would go to the Dupuy home to work out with the home made weights as they prepared for the levee routine and the new football season.

Coach O.J. Brouillette was smart, good and very well organized. He taught chemistry and biology when he wasn't running his players up and down the levee. Practices would start with stretching, then sprints, then playbook, and then tackling and conditioning on the levee.

"Coach Brouillette was a brilliant man, a great instructor, and he used the training on the levee to instill confidence in his players," says Dupuy.

Despite the multifaceted athletic talent, Dupuy says, "The sport that I always go back to is football because that's where I got the discipline."

Six-man was built on speed and toughness. A guy might weigh 135 but coming full speed down the levee he seemed more like 200.

It wasn't just tackling that was practiced on the levee. The quarterback would stand at the top and throw to receivers who were running downhill routes.

It was common practice at the time to deny players water during practices even in extreme heat. This lead to some adaptations at the levee.

Dupuy recalls, "A lot of guys would go down and put water bottles at the bottom of the levee so that when they got there they could take some water. We got caught doing that one time and from then on there was always a coach stationed at the top of the levee to watch what we were doing when we went down the back side of it."

Coach Brouillette used three ball clubs. Dupuy was third string quarterback in his first season and played in the first game. Character is built whenever a coach trusts and believes in you.

"In my first game the first time I carried the ball I gained 15 yards. I also probably had the best punt of my career," remembers Dupuy who went on to become a high school athletic standout gaining a total of sixteen letters in athletics and earning a basketball scholarship to Southeastern. He was also subsequently instrumental in bringing pro baseball to Baton Rouge.

Despite the multifaceted athletic talent, Dupuy says, "I always go back to is football because that's where I get the discipline from."

In fact, Dupuy's dad didn't want him to play football. This wasn't because he needed him to work down on the farm as has been the case in other stories but because he was so athletically talented, especially at baseball.

There were no organized sports in elementary school but Dupuy did play baseball and recalls hitting a grand slam home run against a local rival to win the championship of the West Baton Rouge Parish Fair. So when the possibility of playing football arose, daddy wasn't excited. Far from it.

"My dad worked with a former professional baseball player from the Milwaukee Braves organization who told my dad, 'don't let that kid play football, he's got a chance to play professional baseball and he's going to get hurt playing football,'" L.J. recalls.

Dupuy started off as the six-man team waterboy and then planned to be the trainer, but the allure of the game was simply too much. Apart from the competition, the excitement surrounding the game had always caught L.J.'s imagination.

"People would sit in their cars and when a touchdown was scored they'd blow their horns and flash their lights. You can imagine how much that impressed a first or second grader," he says with a smile.

His father actually didn't realize his son was on the team until the players ran out onto the field for their first game of the season.

"In those days all the cars came and lined around the field and there was a huge following. Everybody made a line for the players to run through and I'm the last one to come out and I've got a uniform on. My daddy wasn't very happy that I was out there with the football team," recalls Dupuy.

Roy Mouch, who had a short-lived career on the initial 1949 six-man team, remembers the cars lined up around the field.

"When we traveled, we traveled in automobiles. Our games were almost all on the road because we didn't have a football field of our own at the time," says Mouch.

Home games were actually played at neighboring Port Allen until 1960 when Brusly got their own field.

"We played St. Gabriel in the third game and I broke my collarbone and that put me out for the season," says Mouch. "I also remember people making tackles and losing their front teeth. Three or four of my buddies right now have false teeth."

Of course, injuries were common, especially when you consider the ferocity of the hitting and the lack of protective gear.

L.J. Dupuy recalls, "When I started playing we had a cardboard helmet with a leather strap in the middle of it. As soon as you finished practice, you'd fold it up, put it in your pocket and head home." Perhaps it was no surprise that his daddy wanted to keep him off the field.

Rodney Prejean, a defensive back and kicker on the 1949 and 1950 teams, later mayor and broadcaster says, "When we got hurt whoever we had acting as a helper would give us a drink but we really didn't have a lot of medical attention."

Dupuy himself separated his shoulder in his senior year and missed most of the season. He also suffered a concussion in the homecoming game of his junior season, one of three that he suffered that season.

Playing against St Joseph of Jeanerette, Dupuy suffered a concussion on the very first play.

"We went through the whole first quarter running the same play. Nobody knew I had a concussion. I still don't remember anything about the game. We were running the same play to our big full back Bobby Allen."

The repetitive play calling worked because each time Allen would gain at least fifteen yards or score a touchdown. Dupuy also intercepted a pass and flipped it to a team-mate who scored a touchdown. He was, however, getting progressively worse.

"I was doing things that weren't natural to me. They realized something was wrong and pulled me. They bought me into the dressing room and said I was fighting the showers when they turned them on," Dupuy recounts.

"It probably happened on kickoff. That was my third concussion that year. People ended up with concussions. You went back in the game. You didn't take seven days off. When you got knocked out they threw you back in the game," L.J . recalls

But sometimes, the injuries were inflicted by the hard-hitting Panthers.

Donald Morales was a halfback and linebacker as well as headhunter on special teams. One time he delivered a particularly big hit.

Randall 'Mule' Miller was a big guy who played for Woodland.

"I tackled him head on in a punt return. He got knocked silly and I got up and went about my business. After the game he invited me into the locker room. I didn't have any idea what the deal was, I wasn't sure what it was about but I went to meet him. He just wanted to shake my hand because he said I had hit him harder than anyone had ever hit him," says Morales.

Morales who started all four years in high school and made all-state his last two years says about football, "What I mostly learned from football was discipline. You had to be on time. You had to do what you had to do, it worked on my life."

However, that didn't stop Morales from breaking a rule or two in his high school days.

The most famous occasion came when some boys at Brusly challenged  local rivals Plaquemine, who had a good eleven-man team with several all-state players, to an improvised game of six-man.

"We broke into our gym and stole the uniforms. We beat them 42-0 and  they formed a fond respect for six-man and for us after that."

The game was played on a Sunday and had a referee. But Morales and others were benched for the first half of the next game for breaking into gym.

L.J. Dupuy also wasn't always the best of students, either. He'd often get into trouble and be sent to the Principal. On one early trip to the Principal's office L.J. recalls the principal telling him, "'Mr. Dupuy meet Mr. Meter.' He pulled a meter stick out and gave me four licks. Later, in a music class, we were breaking pencils and were sent to the Principal again. 'How many pencils did you break? Two, so I got two licks. Nobody else broke pencils but they all got a lick anyway."

But neither Dupuy nor Morales were strangers to hard work. Morales was often up at five to feed the animals, ready for school by 6:30 and in the classroom by 7:30. He recalls that lunch was at 11:50.

"Ms. Tullier from Addis was one of the cooks. Everybody had good food. They were decent meals. There weren't any throwaways like you see now. The ball players looked like they were getting more because they were playing ball. The cooks would pile it on," he says.

The Panthers piled it on during the 1960 season. They lost their first game against St Gabriel but then ran the board ending the season with a tough 18-6 victory against Rougon, which gave the Panthers a 5-1 regular season record.

"Mike Melancon our center was pleading to get the ball. We hadn't thrown it to him all day. So sure enough I threw a hook pass and he caught it to seal the game," says Dupuy.

Dupuy recalls another close game against Rougon in 1960. The Panthers were trying to mount a scoring drive that would have won the game. Unfortunately, the Panthers dropped four passes and narrowly lost. After the game there was a commotion. L.J. Dupuy explains.

"We were heading towards the bus and we heard this huge commotion coming from the graveyard. There seemed to be some fighting and screaming. As we got closer we saw that it was some of the Rougon guys and they were fighting over some girl."

But that was two years in the future as Brusly prepared to play the championship game.

L.J. Dupuy recalls, "I played in the state championship game. We played St Gabriel at the beginning of the 1958 season and lost and then met them again in the championship game. They had an outstanding ball club."

There were no playoffs so the top two teams in the league met for the championship.

"All that week was a big prep thing. We had people from the community watching the practices and you knew it was a big thing. It was the greatest experience of my life," says L.J.

"We had great leaders. Donny Labauve was a favorite of mine. He was the quarterback and later became a CPA. He was tough as a senior leader."

"We ran plays but didn't have a play book per se, up until our senior year when we had a numbering system. But we didn't need it too much. We ran basic plays and were good at them. Coach just had a system."

Brusly basically ran two different offensive sets. One was a T-formation, where the quarterback was under center, received the ball and either handed it off or went straight back for the pass. The other was the closed wing formation where the ball was centered to one of the halfbacks who would hand it to the quarterback, who then became a halfback who could throw the ball or run the option.

"I enjoyed running the double reverse because we had real quick players during my time, like George Elliott, Sanders Thibodeaux, and Donald Morales. On the double reverse the running back could fly around the end and if he turned the corner there wasn't anybody there to stop him," explains Dupuy.

St. Gabriel had beaten Brusly 40-6 in the opening game of the season and so the Panthers' Coaches O.J. Brouillette and Assistant Coach H. Couvillion decided to change things up for the championship game.

"So we split our ends out. Instead of being the three man line tight, we'd split the ends out wide with the anticipation we'd be able to block down and get our guys outside, or if they played outside our ends, we'd go up the middle. It didn't work out. St Gabriel was too fast and we couldn't get outside those guys to block them or couldn't hold off the inside to throw a pass. We couldn't get the passes off because they were on the quarterback before he could get rid of the ball because there wasn't anyone there blocking for him," says Dupuy recalling the 20-0 defeat.

Despite the defeat there was a special moment to savor for the players after the championship game. At that time, there were no pre- or post-game meals. Everyone had to fend for himself.

"After the championship game our Principal Mr. Lousteau took us to Hoppers and bought us a meal. It was like, 'Man, what is this all about!' This is the biggest thing in the world! We thought we were now professional players because we actually had a meal after the game that was paid for by the principal. It was a big deal," says Dupuy.

Dupuy would later become a pro scout for both the Dodgers and Yankees and was instrumental in bringing professional baseball to Baton Rouge with the introduction of the Baton Rouge River Bats. He is presently the head baseball coach at Baton Rouge Community College.

"Brusly always had great administrators. My Principal, Mr. Plaisance, was a strict disciplinarian but a very educated man who employed great teachers who really cared about their students. After him, C.J. Lousteau was a great man, too, especially when it came to athletics. He helped us get what we needed but he also made sure that we got the discipline we needed to be great citizens," says Dupuy.

Dupuy thinks that some important things have been lost since his high school playing days.

"We had parents who cared about us enough to make sure we did things that we were supposed to, both by the bible and the law. I'd like to see better parental guidance at home. It all starts at home. If there's a plea that we can make from six-man nation it would be for parents to take more responsibility at home and work with their kids, bring them up with discipline and bring them up God-fearing. Our country will be better off for it."

Roy Mouch who volunteered and served two years in Korea says, "I think one of the greatest things is playing against someone to see how good or bad you were, what you could or couldn't do, and you learned a lot of things playing football."

But perhaps one of the most enduring and endearing images of the Brusly six-man era comes form L.J. Dupuy, a multi-sport athlete whose father didn't want him to play football.

He recalls scoring his first touchdown after his long layoff because of the dislocated shoulder.

"The quarterback gave me the handoff. I took off and I got hit. My hand went to ground but as I was falling I looked toward the sideline and I saw my dad running down the sideline with me. When I looked up and saw my dad, I bounced off the tackler, stayed off the ground and ended up scoring. When I got to the end zone my dad was running into it, too. He had such joy on his face. It was an unforgettable moment."

-----------------

The Panthers Roster in the 1958 season

Left Ends: Paul Lousteau, Andrew Monk, Lloyd Elwood, W.J. Demarest
Centers: E.J. Tullier, Landess Hebert, Teddy Melancon, David Spears
Right Ends; Sanford DeJean, Hubert Berthelot, Glenn Prejean, Alfred Halphen
Halfbacks; George Elliot, Allen Aillet, Sanders Thibodeaux
Quarterbacks: Donald LaBauve, Bill Tullier, L.J. Dupuy
Fullbacks: Joe LaBauve, Alan Daniels, M.J. Tullier

Coach: O.J. Brouillette
Assistant Coach; H. Couvillion

Best team record: 1950 (8-1)

Confirmed All State Players:

Jim Thibodeaux (Half Back) 1950

Wayne Dupuy (End)- 1954 and 1955

Aldredge (Buttie) Tullier (QB)– 1955

Morris Strauss (Full Back) – 1956

James Sarradett (Half Back) – 1956

Sanders "Skeeter" Thibodeaux (Half Back) – 1959 (Skeeter scored 22 touchdowns in the 1959 season. He joined the military and was a star halfback on the all service football team).

Donnie Morales (Half Back) – 1961 and 1962

Mike Melancon (End/Full Back) – 1962 and 1963 (Mike received a football scholarship to Memphis State after graduating from Brusly)

Junior Hebert (End) – 1964 (Junior played six- man and eight-man and was on the 1964 eight-man All State Team)

David Ocmand (QB) – 1964 and 1965 (David played six-man in the 1963 season and eight- man football in the 1964 season. He scored a school record 27 touchdowns in 1964, including 8 touchdowns against Simmesport, a game Brusly won 86-25. David broke Sanders Thibodeaux's school record of 22 touchdowns, which was set in the 1959 season).

Brusly High School six-man team 1958

# A Concussion, a Homecoming Queen, and a Football Legend

## McKowen Rebels

Six-man football provided and opportunity for small schools to compete athletically despite meager or even non-existent resources. Schools, teams and players all improvised so they could take the field at the weekends during the fall to share in their football experience. The McKowen Rebels provide great examples of how small communities adapted to forge a football tradition. Mckowen High, located in Jackson, Louisiana, was one of only two recognized schools in East Feliciana Parish, which was founded in 1815 as Jackson parish. The McKowen name came about through recognition of land donated to build the school by the McKowen family, of Jackson. The town of Jackson, a major commercial and educational center, was originally named "Bear Corner" but the name changed after General Andrew Jackson and his troops marched through there after the Battle of New Orleans.

McKowen played six-man in the thirties and early forties but their program was transformed with the arrival of Coach C.L. Starnes in 1947. Starnes was a towering figure that demanded the best from every one on his teams. Starnes, who went to Northwestern State University on a basketball scholarship, made the 1937 football team at Northwestern State despite never having played any competitive, organized football. In 1972, he was elected into the school's Graduate Club Athletic Hall of Fame.

Sonny Harris, a star in the early Coach Starnes era, says the coach was, "a prince of a guy, a no bullshit guy. We thought we had died and gone to Heaven because now we could play serious stuff. We now had our coach and leader." Upon his arrival, Coach Starnes organized a few scrimmages against bigger schools like Clinton and Denham Springs. This was a huge difference from the earlier years. The "McKowen Rebels" were now in a positive transition.

The coach may have been great but other resources were in short supply. For one thing there weren't many players. Equipment and uniforms were also hard to come by.

T.W. Pruett, who played offensive and defensive end in the late forties, remembers that, "I went out to practice in the summer and there were six returning members and I was the only new one to show up. They scrimmaged against me and a tackling dummy during defense drills. Coach Starnes bawled me out every time I didn't make a tackle. It was kind of hard. The dummy didn't do his job. He kept moving out of position too many times."

There was a scramble for equipment. We'd get gear from wherever we could. I wore the hip pads that the great Y.A. Tittle had worn at LSU," he says. "We supplemented some equipment with our own earned money."

The equipment that was somehow obtained was less than ideal.

G.D. Spillman, considered by many as the team's 'go-to' guy, recalls the struggle to get uniforms and the unusual means of acquiring new ones.

"We played football with a sweatshirt and number painted on. When we played Mt. Herman they bought us some new shirts," says Spillman.

At various times, the players had to supplement their uniforms with their own money. Spillman, for example, worked in the state hospital in the summer and claims "they hired a lot of kids". In Spillman's senior year he had a construction job.

George Dugas, who played in the early forties, also recalls the problem getting uniforms and his own particular issue.

"We didn't have uniforms except those left over by the people before. We managed to scramble through and get some uniforms that were stored underneath the high school. After that, we supplemented those with our own money that we earned where we could to buy uniforms."

George, however, was a measly 90 pounds even as a 15 year-old and couldn't get any uniforms that fit.

"I got some money to buy some shoulder pads and kneepads from Sears Roebuck," he says.

"We didn't have any masks on our leather helmets," remembers Sonny Harris. Actually, there were only one or two plastic helmets for the entire team. "In the championship game I got gang tackled and I landed face down in a huge puddle and I couldn't breathe. I was splattered in thick mud. I thought I was going to drown."

Coach Starnes came onto the field to check if his star player was okay.

"He asked me if I was okay. I said 'Yeah.' He said, 'get up,' and that I did."

George Dugas recalls his experiences playing in the backfield in 1941 and 1942.

"We didn't have any such thing as a playbook or plans. We told each other what we were going to do in the backfield or the huddle, and then we executed the play. We were all just friends playing."

Dugas recalls that students had to participate in multiple sports. He excelled at track and in boxing. Dugas started school when he was just five years old and boxed through the 1930s. Boxing was a big deal.

"We're talking about 'pee wee' fights, boxing gloves bigger than the kids fighting. Everybody was real proud of what they were doing. Moms and dads would come out and watch the fight go on," says Dugas.

Other family members also encouraged the young Dugas.

"I had an uncle who used to sit in the front row and he had a bunch of nickels in his pocket and he would just rattle them damn nickels, and if I won the fight I got the nickels, so I had an incentive. In the 30s, if you wore your Boy Scout uniform you got in for free," recalls Dugas.

Sonny Harris also recounts having to participate in other sports.

"To keep playing football you had to play other sports. As much as I hated baseball and really needed to be working in the summer, I played baseball so I could play football. Then there was basketball and track. Some of us lettered in all four sports! It was a great life and as a kid I did good to keep going. I was the first kid in Jackson to get an Eagle Scout medal. The town sponsored my trip to the BSA National Jamboree in Valley Forge, PA. Life was wonderful!"

With Coach Starnes at the helm and some games under their belt, the 1948 Rebels were ready to compete.

"The players wanted to use the new "T" formation some of the competitive teams were using for our offense, but coach wouldn't buy it, we had to use the old 'single wing' formation," said Sonny Harris.

TW Pruett remembers that, "1948 was our best season. We went to the championship and lost by one point."

"We split two games with Dutchtown and had to have a play-off. It was raining so hard; the field was full of water. When you tackled somebody you held his head up so he wouldn't drown. The last play before halftime the officials placed the ball at midfield and it floated away. A gust of wind picked up some cars on the sidelines and flopped them around. They called the game off at that time. We had to come back the next week."

Doyle Harrell, who played center, remembers some of the game against Dutchtown.

"They had a guy called Johnson, a big fullback. He was coming through the middle and I was going to see if I couldn't put the hit of all times on him. I came in real hard and he was coming for me with his knees high and as I ducked I caught a knee right over my right eye," remembers Harrell.

These were long before the days of "concussion protocols" or even recognition of the signs and seriousness of head injuries.

Harrell got up, shook himself off and went into the huddle.

The Wrong One!

"I got up and went into the Dutchtown huddle. They said, 'No, No, No, you've got to go.'"

There was a doctor on the sidelines and he reviewed Harrell's faculties.

"Dr. McAdams said I'd be OK. Coach Starnes asked me whether I felt okay enough to go back in. I said, 'Sure, I'd love to go back in.' He said 'ok,' so I went to get a helmet."

Doctors may still have had a lot to learn about concussions but moms will always be moms.

"When I went to get my helmet, that was when my mother -- a little fat lady -- came out of the stands. 'No, no, no!' she yelled, 'He's through for the night!' So I didn't go back and play anymore that night."

Harrell also remembers the storm-affected game against Dutchtown.

"It started storming and the rain washed out the markings on the field. At one point Dutchtown scored and they had to take the yard marker to measure out from the goal post to see if they had actually crossed the line. I think the score was tied at half time so they called the game."

The proud rebels were now ready to introduce their first homecoming queen, Ms. Lucille Fluker, about the time the storm was at its worst. Lucille had a homemade crown covered in foil. The home economics teacher made the rosebud corsage she wore. She was "beautiful!" Lucille recalling the experience said she was escorted on the field, not in a convertible, but on foot by the captain of the football team, G. D. Spillman. Lucille recalls, "the weather was horrible, it was muddy, well the lights went out and at half-time the game was postponed." Lucille, a freshman, was the only one in the homecoming court. There were only 50 students in the whole school.

Harrell, the kid with the insistent mom, recalls making a key play in one close game.

"It was towards the end of the game and we were down by just a couple of points. They were going to punt. Fortunately, I got through the line and blocked the punt. We recovered the ball on the 20-yard line."

Surprised by the block, the players were confused as what to do next.

"We didn't know what to do and started looking at the bench. Sonny Harris headed to the sidelines to get some instructions from coach Starnes."

When he came back into the huddle the other five players were anxious to know the plan.

"Sonny got back in the huddle and everyone gathered around and asked him what the coach had said. What did he say? Sonny looked up and said, 'SCORE.' And we did, and we won the game."

If the coach was a man of few words, he was also stingy with the pre-game meal.

Donald Morrison, who played for the rebels recalls, "We'd get near the game and the coach would hand us a dollar to get something to eat. He didn't want us to eat too much and get sick during the game."

Marvin McConnell recalls another occasion where the coach's anorexic plans were stymied.

"On the way to Gonzales we stopped at a restaurant and ate the small amount that the coach ordered. On the way out of the restaurant, however, a bread truck came by the back door and a few loaves fell out on the floor. We ran over, picked them up and gorged on them."

Starving or not, the 1948 team were very competitive. They ran up some big scores.

G.D. Spillman recalls that, "A lot of teams were whipped so bad that coach took me out after we had got so far ahead."

"G.D. was our top performer. He could do it all," says Sonny Harris.

But G.D. wasn't the only star performer. There were other players who performed at championship level game after game.

Dickie Turnipseed, playing quarterback, was a force to be reckoned with. Bobby Dugas could run the ball against the best defenses. Tom Graves, with his height and speed, was a champion end.

Sonny Harris was a star on that team, too.

"I played behind G.D. Spillman and the big guys and I did play in that championship game, got the **** kicked out of me."

In that championship game, Spillman scored five touchdowns in a heart breaking 37-36 loss against St. Martinville, a school who had 60 players available.

For Marvin McConnell losing in heart breaking fashion wasn't the only injury.

"In the championship game somebody threw a block on my left knee and put me out of commission. The most miserable part was that I had to drive home in my '37 Ford with a standard manual transmission. I couldn't raise my left leg up so I had to push the clutch down and pop it with my right foot, but we got home alright," remembers Marvin.

Despite the championship loss, everyone who played for McKowen took something positive away from their experience that transcended football.

Billy Smith was anxious to play even when he was still in the sixth grade. Coach asked him to be the equipment manager, a task he duly performed for four years. When his chance to play did come in tenth grade he played quarterback and safety.

"I touched the ball six times that season and scored on each play. I loved playing defense. I weighed 125 but I was big enough nobody was too big or mean for me to knock down," says Smith.

Smith says that Starnes taught him determination and toughness.

"One time, I fell out of a deer stand, crawled a quarter mile with a broken hip, pulled myself into my pickup drove myself out of the woods to get help. I probably wouldn't have been able to do that if it hadn't been for Coach Starnes," says Smith.

Marvin McConnell also observed discipline of a different type while playing.

"We had a little facility behind the school. It had no showers or anything. We'd dress out, workout, go back and get dressed. The little building was also used for something else."

What was it used for? Workouts? Weight Training? Secret team meetings?

"It was where the Principal John Harris, Sr., would take the big boys that had been bad and kind of reprimand them real seriously. He would reprimand them with a good lick on the rear with the belt and he sure knew how to use it."

The total football experience stood most of team members in good stead. Many of them accomplished much in their lives after football. The discipline learned, the dedication exhibited, the team spirit, all helped develop potential and a sense of service

Sonny Harris wanted to go to LSU as engineer.

Somewhere along the way someone gave him the idea that, "You don't have the brains to be in agriculture much less engineering." So, Sonny joined the Navy. He finished in the top five in an electronics course and served the rest of his military time as an electronic technician aboard a submarine.

Tom Graves played in championship game against St Martinsville. He ran the hundred in 10.4. Afterwards, he went to LSU and worked in the training room under legendary trainer Marty Broussard. He attended medical school in New Orleans and then became a navy flight surgeon.

Other examples of success can be found in the McKowen "High Hall of Distinction" noting individuals and their accomplishments. There are many who were former 'six-man' team players; business owners, a dermatologist, a VP of Marketing for a major company, two Superintendents of Education, and the homecoming queen who became a spokesperson for a fortune 500 company.

Perhaps Billy Smith summed it up the best. "The years at McKowen were the greatest years of my life." Billy Smith, earned a Ph.D.in Education and is a former Dean of Education of the College Education at Louisiana State University.

In the broad scope of Louisiana football history there is an additional note of football greatness. One of East Feliciana parish's most famous favorite sons is Eddie Robinson, the second winningest coach in NCAA Division 1 football.

For a staggering 57 years, Robinson was the coach of Grambling, a historically black university in Louisiana. Robinson started his career while six-man football was the tradition in the state. He graduated from Leland College with a bachelor's degree and returned to New Orleans and took a job in a feed mill. His dreams of becoming a football coach seemed unlikely, given these were the days of segregation. But shortly after he took the mill job he heard that Louisiana Negro Normal and Industrial Institute (the precursor of Grambling) was looking for a football coach and the rest is history.

Between 1960 and 1990 Coach Robinson only had one losing season! Grambling has named its football facility in his honor and the Football Writers Association of America have an award also named in after him. In 1985, Robinson received the Alonzo Stagg Award in recognition of his outstanding achievement as a coach. The legendary Joe Paterno said, "Our profession will never, ever be able to repay Eddie Robinson for what he has done for the country and the profession of football."

Coach Robinson would have been familiar with the small school culture of McKowen and rural Louisiana schools in general.

McKowen team of 1958. Bottom, left to right: Rish, Jolks, Peterson, Aldredge, DeLaune, Hetcher, Reynolds, Rodgers. Top: Darthy, Hudson, Parker, Hawes, Vernon, Weaver, Howell

# A Convincing Fake, Convicts and a Championship

## St. Gabriel Broncos

St. Gabriel is another story of a small school that punched above its weight and won two six-man championships. It benefitted from a great coach and the pre- and post World War II values that permeated the small community.

St Gabriel is twelve miles east of Baton Rouge and sits on the east bank of the Mississippi river. The town, which was incorporated in 1994, has a total area of 29 square miles. The 2000 census recorded approximately 5500 residents.

Coach Herb 'Run' Hernandez graduated from Rayne High School where he played quarterback in the 1941-42 school year, and spent a year at LSU before volunteering for the Marine Corps, where he spent three years mostly in the Pacific theater, notably Iwo Jima and Saipan as part of the U.S. Army occupation of Japan.

The coach earned the nickname "run" because, according to one of his players Jimmy Taylor, "He had better not catch you walking anywhere." He was an assistant coach at Ville Platte for one year before moving on to coach at St. Gabriel where he won two six-man championships in 1957 and 1958. He later coached for White Castle where he won the 1967 eight-man state championships. In 2010 he was nominated for the Louisiana High School Athletic Association Hall of Fame.

Coach Hernandez has a slightly different take on six-man than many. Although he admits games were wide open, he believes that if you emphasized defense, you could hold the opponents to relatively low scoring games.

"Six-man is not necessarily wide open if you emphasize defense. I can remember two games with Woodland where both times the score was 8-6. In one of those games I recall that one team had eight first downs, the other five," he says.

"The end was the key to your defense because most teams ran wide. They ran outside. They didn't really come up the middle," says the coach.

But trickery was a key to springing players loose and once the sprinters did get free they'd almost always score. Coach Hernandez recalls a fake that worked too well.

"We ran a fake play and the referee lost the ball. He followed the kid who was the fake. He goes up to the kid and says 'give me the ball.' The kid says, 'I ain't got the ball. But I tell you what, if you look at the fellow in the end zone right there, he's got the ball!' Unfortunately, the ref had blown the play dead and the touchdown didn't count! In fairness, he came over to the sideline and apologized," recalls the coach.

Hernandez pays tribute to the hard work and values of the times in general and the area in particular.

A lot of the kids at St. Gabriel were hard working. Many grew up on farms and worked the fields as well as their textbooks and playbooks.

"A lot of those kids came up the hard way and they appreciated stuff," says the coach.

That hard work meant working the fields immediately after school and then coming back for evening practice.

"Price Leblanc was a cattle farmer and he would park his truck by the school. At about 3pm, as school let out, five or six players would jump in his truck and go pick hay. They'd work the fields for him until practice time around six," says Hernandez.

"We'd practice at night so they could work in the afternoon."

Mostly, the kids didn't complain, just followed orders and did what was necessary. One time, a player showed up ready to get on the bus for a road game.

"The kid needed a haircut. I looked at him and said 'you're not coming with me.' He took off and had the quickest haircut on record and was back just in time to get on the bus before we left!"

Coach says he rarely recalled discipline problems. On the contrary, his players and students did what was asked of them without demur. Sometimes the demands on them came from unexpected circumstances.

"We're coming up the bridge in Baton Rouge going to Plaquemine. We had to floor it to get up to the bridge. We just made it. We got to Plaquemine and had to stop for a red light and the motor died. I told the kids 'Well, y'all have to get out and push the bus so we can start'. So I had about 15 or 20 kids pushing the bus and it started and we made it home."

Coach recalls some great players in his time. One was from St. Gabriel.

"I had a quarterback who was a ninth-grader. He weighed a hundred pounds and played for four years. He got tackled once in his entire playing career. His name was Allen Landaiche," says the coach about one of the stars on his 1958 championship team.

St. Gabriel had actually won the championship when coach was getting home from the war in 1946.

Like many schools that year, St. Gabriel had people returning from the war to complete their high school education.

"The year we won the state championship, 1946, we had a lot of fellows coming back from the war and finishing their last year of high school. We had quite a few big guys here at the time. They were almost fully grown men," recalls L.G. Hoffman a running back on the 1946-1950 Bronco teams.

During Hoffman's playing years, Verney Becnel was the coach and L.J.'s dad, L.G. Sr., was the assistant. They didn't practice much because most boys had to go home, help around the farm and milk the cows. They practiced about four or five hours a week.

L.G. Sr. had a model A Ford that drove his son around town but away games meant sitting on a bus with wooden benches.

Hoffman recalls, "Most games were no further than Gonzales or St. Amant, about twenty to twenty-five miles away. Uncle Charlie owned the bus and he wouldn't let anyone else drive it."

But the post-war years were lean, except for 1946.

"Some years we only had about 10 or 12 guys on the team. One year it was only eight but we beat Gonzales that year," recalls Hoffman. But they also get whipped a few times.

"We had a lot of sixties and seventies scored against us. For us it was just a nice way to spend leisure time is what it amounted to," says L.G.

Sometimes L.G. had to contend with teammates as well as the opponents.

He recalls, "Blue Philippe was a mean little rascal. I'd be up against him and he'd kick me in the shins every time he got up. So I waited one day when he wasn't watching, he got down in his stance and I kicked him as hard as I could in the shin. He ran me all over the school ground but he never did kick me again."

Coach Hernandez has already been quoted as saying defense could be underrated in six-man.

Pat Landaiche who played on the 1958 team, gives some insight into the Bronco's defensive unit.

"Our defensive unit was called the Convicts. LSU had the 'Chinese Bandits' so we came up with a similar name," says Pat.

But that wasn't the only reason for the name.

The St. Gabriel School bordered on a prison farm.

"There were no fences between the inmates and the school population. So, we picked up on the term 'convict' since we thought you must have done something tough or mean to be in prison," says Alan.

The convicts came up big in the championship game. Here is how one paper described the action.

"St. Gabriel won its fifteenth game in a row and second six-man championship Thursday, defeating Brusly 20-0. The Broncos scored mid-way through the first quarter when Errol Cambre ran forty yards for the first touchdown. The kick by Allen Landaiche was no good.

"St. Gabriel received the ball after the half and marched to the Brusly 10 yard line from where Stan Lablanc, on an end around, went over standing up for the second touchdown. The dropkick by Landaiche was good to make it 14-0.

"At the beginning of the fourth quarter, St Gabriel end Lawrence Messina blocked and recovered a Brusly punt on the Brusly five-yard line. Fred Thompson then drove through the center for the score. St Gabriel twice held Brusly inside the 10 yard line."

The Convicts rose to the challenge and proved their coach's philosophy that solid defense could work in the wide open fields of six-man football.

Glen Auton, who played for St. Joseph of Jeanerette, is a good friend of Coach Hernandez and to this day he recalls his time playing for St. Josephs.

"At St. Josephs, we threw the football a lot more than most. Our quarterback was Allen Breaux and today he is a priest at the Catholic Church in Scott, Louisiana."

But Glen also has something important to say about coaches like Coach Hernandez who shaped the lives of so many of the students he coached.

"Everybody who played any kind of sports had coaches and a lot of these coaches were like fathers. These young men and women throughout life grew up in their father's image and in their coaches' image. It's great what all the coaches really did for the kids. I know it wasn't done for the money and it took a lot of time. So, on behalf of all people who played sports, I want to thank all the coaches because it's been a great run," says Glen.

---

St Gabriel All-State 1959 selections in their championship season...
Allen Landaiche QB 1st team
Austin Kinchen C 1st
David Broussard E 2nd team
Benny Daigle C 2nd team
Errol Cambre H 2nd
Fred Thompson H 2nd

White Castle's outstanding players for Coach Hernandez six-man teams.

E.L. Gueho (First two time All State Player at two different positions)
O.J. Landry (First All State player in school history)
Larry Hymel (Scored first TD at White Castle)
Coonie Caillet (Scored school record 7 TDs in one game)

St. Gabriel "Convicts," 1958. From left: Fred Thompson, Lawrence Messina, Austin Kinchen, Pat Landiche, David Broussard, Eroyl Cambre.

Line, left to right: Roy Gomez, Webb Harelson, Bobby Fairchild. Back field: L.G. Hoffmann, Donald LeBlanc, Lawrence Crochet.

# Coach K, Resilience, and Roast, Toast, Taters and Tea

## Woodland Bulldogs

Woodland High school has a proud tradition in six-man football having won three consecutive state championships in 1959, 1960 and 1961. It switched to eight-man football shortly thereafter and won the 1967 championship. As in many of these stories, the coach is a central figure, instilling a tough discipline and resilience that showed itself both on and off the field.

St Helena parish was originally part of western Florida but when that state gave up its claims to the Louisiana land in 1810, it assimilated into Louisiana. The parish has an area of more than 400 square miles and, during the 1950's and 1960s, had a population of about 9,000. It's dairy farming country.

At the center of this story is Coach J.O. Kuyrkendall.

Quarterback Chris Davis who played on the 1967 eight-man championship team was quite an athlete who featured as quarterback but was also an all-star defensive back, too. He started playing in the seventh grade because there were very few students in the school. In fact there were only 18 students in the graduating class. But starting out early helped.

"A lot of kids played in the ninth grade so we played a lot together, which helped as we progressed and eventually we won the championship hands down," says Chris, now an accomplished artist who lives on the very dairy farm, located by the upper Tickfaw River, where he grew up.

"Coach Kuyrkendall was our coach. He had a board that was long and had holes in it and if you got out of line, he was swinging for the fence. It hurt. He was old school," remembers Chris.

Coach K was so old school that he had a special drill for those who messed up in one way or another. Chris explains.

"If you messed up out on the field, or missed your block, if you weren't hustling, he would take two lineman -- and this is in front of the crowd -- and h would make y'all run head-on into each other like a practice, right there in front of the crowd. That kind of inspired a lot of guys, because nobody wanted to be doing that in front of their family and the whole community. Or the cheerleaders."

It was clear that the coach got the job done and his results speak for themselves.

"He would never get away with that kind of stuff today with the psychologists and lawsuits," says Chris. "But he was a very interesting man, a very colorful fellow and a big influence on all of us."

Tommy Hulsey, whose dad was the principal and who lived with the bachelor coach for three years in his elementary school years, also remembers the 'sideline drill'.

"He lined up two people and you had to hit each other head on until he blew the whistle. You'd make good contact then get back in your stance and he just kept doing it until you couldn't do it any more. It really didn't matter to him. He'd do it before, during the game at half time, whenever. The sideline drill definitely worked. You didn't want to be doing it in front of your fans," says Tommy, who played the last season of eight-man football at Woodland.

Coach wasn't just a stickler about football.

Tommy, who was given the nickname "Tiger" by the coach, recalled an incident going to a road game.

"We were going to Simmsport and I was in the ninth grade. We took the ferry and there was a gravel truck right there, so we took some rocks. We're going down the road in the bus and as a sign comes up, we reached out the window, threw the rocks to pop the sign. We did this a couple of times and Coach K heard it. So we got to Simmsport and I had to do the sideline drill in front of everyone include my daddy, the Principal. My daddy asked the coach, "What's going on?" Coach said it was just a little sideline drill that's all," Tommy recalls.

Practice was hot and the coach would get on a sled and make the boys push him up and down a hill.

"Coach would get on the back of the sled. We would push that thing up and down the old hill there and hated every minute of it. Then we had to run wind sprints," says Chris Davis.

But the hard practice taught some very valuable life lessons.

"You learn teamwork. Running sprints, or sideline drills. If you were on your own you'd quit long before but when the whole team is there you just keep going," says Tommy, a sentiment echoed by Chris.

One day in the midst of a tough practice, Chris came to an important realization. The boys were all running wind sprints and if anybody dragged their feet the whole team would have to run an extra circuit.

"I never forget it. It must have been 97 out there and I was sitting down, on my knees, puking, and we were all on the goal line and I thought to myself, 'I'm a little bitty fella at 145 pounds and I can run to that goal line without too much trouble but Jerry Jenkins, one of our classmates, weighs 250 pounds plus and it must be way harder on him.' At that moment I think I learned something valuable for the rest of my life; don't gripe because there's always somebody who has got it a whole lot worse than you," says Chris.

Often, these dairy farmers' sons had to go home after practice and work on the farm.

"We were farmers' sons and most of us had to milk the cows so we usually had to milk cows after practice. Sometimes we would swing by Hillsdale Bridge and jump in the water to cool off," says Chris.

Cary Travis, who played on the eight-man team and backed up Chris Davis says, "I remember coming home to milk cows then going back for the game. I came from an era when my dad died I was young, raised by my stepfather and he was from the World War II generation and it was 'yes sir, no sir,'" says Cary.

Leonard Addison was from a different era and didn't play at Woodland although some of his teammates from Pine Grove did. Pine Grove played one season of eight-man in 1955 and three games in 1956.

"The boys that had some eligibility left went to play at Woodland. I didn't go. It was rough. Sometimes I'd get back from a game at midnight, then get up at 4 to milk cows."

Leonard recalls the pitfalls of having a very small school.

"The last game we played was against Livonia. We were playing so bad that the coach had us practice at halftime instead of talking to us. The very first play of the second half, we kicked off, I made a tackle and I broke a tooth. I think that's when the Principal decided to call it quits. We only had seven men suited up. We only had twelve in my senior class and the following year there was six."

Paul Thompson played on the three six-man championship teams.

"Uniforms had to be neat, clean and tucked in. If you walked on the field with your shirt untucked, you'd be sent back to the bench. It didn't matter what position you played," says Paul.

Shoes had to be polished and shoestrings had to be clean for every game.

"For those of us who were playing, we spent most of the day getting ready for the night, getting our uniforms ready, shoes shined, getting new shoestrings or getting them cleaned. That was basically what we did all day. Then we'd have our pregame meal, which was prepared by our cheerleaders, and then it would be time to take a nap on the mat," says Paul about the game day routine.

The meal prepared by the cheerleaders was 'Roast, Toast, Taters, and Tea.'

Chris recalls, "After the meal we were meant to sleep but there was always something going on and coach would sneak by and peep in and if you weren't sleeping that board was waiting for you."

Cary Travis remembers that the "potatoes were home made, no instant stuff. And the tea was warm."

Ted Chapman who was a freshman cornerback on the 1967 eight-man champions recalls the game day ritual.

"Game day was exciting. Everybody was excited. The cheerleaders even wore their uniforms to school. When you come from a small community in St Helena parish, a high school football game was the epitome of the week. It was the climax especially when you're playing at home. You didn't do much schoolwork that day. You mostly just had thoughts of football running through your head."

Chris Davis recalls some of the games in the 1967 championship year.

"We went to Loranger one night and we were goofing off and they scored on us. So Coach K became unglued and we got chewed out real good and then he said I want y'all to roll the quarterback roll, which meant the big guys were in front of me."

It worked. The bug guys wiped out the Loranger defense and Davis ran straight down the sidelines five times for touchdowns.

"My teammates, especially, Johnny McCoy, were teasing me, 'you greedy ball hog!' They would never let me live that down, scoring five touchdowns."

Chris also recalls a pivotal play in the championship game.

"In the state championship game, one play sealed it for us. I was a little guy 5'7" and with big guys rushing I couldn't see over them to throw. Coach came up with this play where we faked it one way and our good running back, Milton Breechen, snuck through the line. I knew he was going to be wide open. All I had to do was to heave it up there over the lineman. Sure enough, I rolled back, they rushed, I couldn't see a thing but I just threw it up there. Once I heard the crowd come unglued, I knew we'd scored a touchdown. That sealed the game and that winning that state championship was a really big thing for us."

Chris also recalls having another meaningful realization after winning the championship.

"I remember saying the Lord's Prayer before every game and then after winning the championship. We put all our hands together and said that prayer, and for the first time I think I realized the power of the team and the value of all the sacrifice we had endured for each other. For us to hold that trophy together was an amazing thing. It showed me what something higher and greater than yourself can mean," says Chris.

Ted Chapman, the freshman cornerback on the 1967 team has an admission about the championship game against Pride.

"I have never told anyone this but before the game I was scared. Pride had a running back that looked like he was 200 pounds, at least he looked that way to me."

That big running back would lead to take out the defensive end, which meant running right at the 140-pound freshman.

"We didn't have linebackers, so it was me and this big running back. I was scared but once he realized I wasn't backing off, they tried the other side. They tried throwing at me and running at me. They thought they could take advantage of me. I did intercept a pass and I think I held my own," says Chapman modestly.

Paul Thompson played between 1959 and 1962 and thus won the championship his first three years.

Paul is a witness to Coach K's willingness to adapt and his concern for his players.

"He took a small group of country boys and made us a team," says Paul.

One night, Woodland was playing Shady Grove, and they had a four man defensive line. The Woodland boys kept running a cross-buck into the line and it simply didn't work. They were being stopped all the time.

"In the middle of the second quarter one of our guys called timeout and said he wanted to talk to the coach and so we went to the bench," recalls Thompson.

"Coach said, 'What do you need Joe?'"

'Well, Coach, you keep wanting us to run a cross-buck against their four man line. But you've told us for two years that a cross-buck doesn't work against a four man line.'

Coach looked at him and said, "You're right, Joe."

"After that we didn't run the cross-buck and about everything we did run worked."

There was an intense rivalry with Albany, and one time Coach K did all he could to protect his players.

"The first time we played, the rivalry was so intense that the coach decided we couldn't go there as normal. He thought it was too dangerous for us to even go in the dressing room. We actually drove the school bus out to the field and parked right by the bench. We got off the bus. We played. At halftime we got back on the bus. When the game was over, we got back on the bus quickly and immediately left. We were told that we would be physically handled if we had won the game. A few fights did break out but none involved the players," says Thompson, who also recalls scoring three touchdowns in another game against Rougon.

Paul Thompson also remembers that the hitting was fierce.

"One of the helmet companies came to our school and gave us six brand new helmets to try out. The first game, we either completely broke every helmet or the straps inside broke, which tells you about the level of contact we were making," says Paul.

Ted Chapman, now an attorney, claims that football made a huge difference in his life.

"I came from a dysfunctional family and Coach K was like a surrogate father to me. Football was my life and a family away from home. Football to me was family," says Chapman

This sense of family made it even more difficult for Chapman when he had to leave Woodland in the eleventh grade. Integration was instituted and many students, especially athletes, went to private schools and Woodland had to terminate its football program.

"I went to New Orleans and played two years at Alcee Fortier Senior High School. It was 4A and I did end up making the district team as a senior. But it was very sad to leave Woodland. I would have rather played out my time and finished there. We grew up there and I went there from the first grade. It was like family. I was very sad leaving there."

Overall, however, football made a massive difference in Chapman's life.

"It gave me confidence in life endeavors. It was family, It gave me normalcy that I wouldn't have otherwise had. I thank God I grew up in that situation. I wished my children and their children would have grown up with the same community standards," says Chapman, whose determination and resilience earned him a law degree, and he has practiced locally for more than 25 years.

Tommy Hulsey also thinks his football lessons helped his career.

"That determination I learned playing football kept me going when I was in Vet school where the other students were just as smart as I was," says Tommy.

Before Chris Davis became an artist he played football at Southwest Mississippi Junior College. When he went out to play he immediately noticed the difference between the eight-man and the eleven-man game.

"I never forget I was playing split end and on the first day of practice I caught a pass out on the sidelines. I was a small guy, 5'7" and 145 when soaking wet. But I was quick on my feet and in eight-man you could dodge round the field all day. Well, they threw me a pass in the flat, I caught it and sure enough I side-stepped the first guy coming through but the next thing I remember was the darnedest wave of grunting and growling, cussing and hollering, and tackling. I got up out of that mess and I said, "Gee whiz, this is different." And that was the difference, there were three more men on the field, which made it a lot smaller. Also, everyone was as fast as I was," says Chris.

Chris also recalls limited supplies of Gatorade and creative ways to slake one's thirst during hot, college practices.

"There was a lot of wheeling and dealing for that Gatorade. They'd also irrigate the field and if you missed a pass you'd go sliding into where they'd watered the field -- and drink right off the grass!"

Obviously, football was more than just a game, not just to the players but to the whole community.

"Football was like a social. It was a form of communication where people talked about what was happening in their lives and kept up with each other. It was a big thing, more than just football. It was a time for renewing friendships and acquaintances," says Chapman.

"Friday nights were a big deal in a small farming community. We were very community oriented and there weren't too many other things to do and many people were poor. When people gathered there was a spirit and a sense of togetherness," says Davis.

"You wanted to be part of that camaraderie," says Travis. "I'm 60 years old and I can honestly say those were some of the best days of my life. I enjoyed every minute and to go back and re-do it, well, I'd do it as fast as I could. We've still got friendships."

"We've stayed in touch and been friends for 45 years."

From left to right: Ted Chapman, Chris Davis, Coach Barrett Murphy, Tom Haulsey, Cary Travis, Paul Thompson.

Paul Thompson and his Woodland High School letterman's jacket.

# A Veteran, A Disinterested Student, and a Helpless Coach

## Basile Bearcats, Bell City Bear Cubs, Creole Pirates

The end of World War II saw the return of many veterans to their home communities to resume their education, their training, their lives. In some cases, returning veterans found themselves in new communities and some had an immediate impact.

Louis Hanson was from upstate New York and had served in the Air Force. He married a girl from Basile, Louisiana, and once he arrived he was charged with trying to start a football program at Basile High School.

Ernie Duplechin lived with his grandmother and three brothers in the country near Basile.

"The three other boys were a little older than I but they never went to school. Going to school was a luxury for those who wanted to go. There was no such thing as *having* to go to school. You were too busy chopping the cotton, shucking rice and whatever else was needed," says Ernie.

Ernie did go to school but wasn't that excited about it. In fact, he'd rather have been working back home with the rest of his family.

"We were poor. We had a little six acre cotton patch that we had to hoe this, that and the other. We'd pick cotton and then here comes the rice cutting. Cutting that row around the field so you could have a place for the tractor without it mashing the rice down."

When Coach Hanson came to town, everything changed for Ernie.

"I was just waiting for a reason to quit school. I didn't like it but he came and convinced me to stay and play football. I fell in love with the sport. I could hit anyone that was out there and not get punished! It was a great turning point in my life," says Ernie.

Ernie, and the other seventeen boys in his *school* had never seen a football. This made for a rough beginning to the Basile six-man program. They lost their first game to Kaplan 76-6 being demolished by Kaplan's star athlete Joe Kite. Mamou trounced the Bearcats the next week but Hanson soon crafted a competitive team.

By his senior season, Duplechin and his teammates were challenging for the championship.

After losing the first game of the season to Buras 28-14, the Bearcats chalked up nine straight wins, scoring more than forty points a game. This took them to the district championship against Lake Arthur whom they beat 55-18. Then it was on to the state championship against rival Buras.

It was an extremely close affair and in the end, decided by the deadly kicking of Silton Aucoin, who kicked three two-point conversions on the way to a 30-28 Basile victory.

"Coach Louis Hanson changed the whole perspective on life in Basile. I've never heard him say a cuss word. There's no telling where I'd be today if it weren't for that man. He started the six-man all-star game right here in Lake Charles in 1950, " recalls Ernie.

Indeed, several of the Basile stars played in the first annual six-man all-star game, initiated by Louis Hanson, who coached the West squad. The Citizen newspaper reported that, "approximately 800 fans contributed more than $750 to the coffers of the Small School Coaches clinic."

Ernie Duplechin was the offensive star of the game, as reported in the Citizen.

"Ernie Duplechin of Basile opened the scoring with touchdown gallops of 20 and 49 yards for the first two western tallies in the first two quarters."

Louis Jeans of Basile also scored late on giving the West a 35-12 victory.

Duplechin comments about his coach.

"Louis Hanson was heck of a coach. He was an awakening for the whole area, not just for the school, the town, but the people. They supported football like crazy."

More than that, Hanson supported Duplechin off the field. Ernie actually lived with the coach for a while. Later, the coach encouraged Ernie to consider leaving Louisiana if he didn't want to risk interruption to his education by a possible call from the National Guard. As it happens, Ernie was drawing attention from colleges outside of the state, including Texas A & M.

Ernie recalls the trip on the train to Houston and from there to College Station. A graduate assistant showed him around and everyone tried to make him feel welcome. On his second day at College Station, he got a call from his buddy Louis Jeans, who was playing in a basketball tournament back home in Louisiana. The next night, Ernie called his buddy Louis again, and the night after.

Each night, Louis and Ernie lamented the fact that Duplechin was so far away and unable to enjoy their sporting exploits together.

"On the Wednesday morning I walked into A&M Coach Tyler's office and told him 'Hey, buddy, you've got a fine place here, I like it, but I'm going home,'" recalls Ernie.

There was another reason for going home.

The future Mrs. Duplechin.

Dolores McClelland loved school because she could be with her friends.

"One of the things we loved to do was to watch six-man games. We loved watching the cheerleaders. At that point we were too young to participate, but I did later become a cheerleader, " says Dolores.

Dolores does remember one of the cheers designed to encourage the team.

""Little red rooster, sitting on a fence, crowing for Basile, he's got sense."

In her junior year, Dolores took a fancy to one of the boys in the school.

"He was a sophomore but I want you to know that he was older than I was," she insists.

Dolores takes up the story.

"I really liked him but he was dating somebody else so I didn't want him to know it. Finally, I heard that he had broken up with this other girl and I said to myself this is my chance now. We got to liking each other and we started dating. I played on the basketball team and he said the reason he asked me to go out with him was because he liked me in my little red basketball uniform. After high school, Ernie and I went to Louisiana College and were married two years later."

Ernie and Dolores had a family of five children, including two boys, one of whom played at McNeese State, which just happens to be where his dad Ernie, ended up coaching.

"Football and coaching was a major part of our life. And we loved every minute of it," say Dolores.

"It was all made possible by Louis Hanson," adds Ernie.

Not far from where Coach Hanson changed Ernie Duplechin's life, something similar was happening with another coach and another disinterested student.

Paul 'Sonny' Arceneaux played six-man football for Bell City from 1950 through 1954.

Sonny explains. "I came from a home that was busted up during the war. I think I changed schools six or seven times. Welsh, New Orleans, then Landry Memorial Catholic, Lake Charles  and Bell City. I knew the fundamentals but I was despondent when I got to Bell City because I had left my friends in Lake Charles."

At that time, Bell City only had a basketball and a track team, no football. But that was about to change. Coach Clarence Theriot approached Sonny one day at school.

"We're thinking of starting football, would you be interested?" the coach asked.

"He couldn't have bought me a Christmas present that was any better than that. From that point on I really started enjoying high school," says Sonny.

The coach encouraged Sonny in all aspects of his life. But that didn't stop him from being tough on the young man.

"I was always diagramming plays, and one time coach really got on me for doing that in class!" recalls Sonny.

Sonny had a tremendous respect for his coach, which led to a memorable incident.

The games against rivals Mamou were big under any circumstances but they were given extra special spice because of one fact.  Coach Theriot's father-in-law was the Principal of Mamou.

"I got together with a couple of my teammates and I said we've just got to try extra hard tonight. We're going to go out and do whatever we need to do. We worked ourselves up into a dither," says Sonny.

So much of a dither, in fact, that Sonny made himself sick.

"I had to go the Coach just before kick-off and tell him I don't feel so good. I've got a headache. He gave me aspirin. Once we started I was all right. We scored quite a bit and won the game 31-6," remembers Sonny.

Sonny's senior season was Bell City's finest, as they went 6-2 and Coach Theriot was named Coach of the Year. Arceneaux was the standout. In that year Sonny had 25 rushing touchdowns and 6 passing TDs.

He always eagerly anticipated games against Welsh, a former school, where he knew many of the players.

"I knew all the players because I had gone to school with them. I remember Pierre Daubaval, Jimmy Lee, James Louvier. I remember this one game, We kicked off and stopped them. They punted and I ran it back for a touchdown!" says Sonny.

The Welsh newspaper called the 60-yard return "the most exciting offensive play of the game."

There were bigger games ahead.

"We played Creole and we were both undefeated at the time. I remember people coming up to me and telling me they had bets on the game so I had better do good," recalls Sonny.

Here's how one newspaper covered the game.

"The Bell City Bear Cubs scored in every quarter to swamp the previously unbeaten Creole Pirates 45-25. This was undoubtedly Bell City's best performance of the year as the blocking was functioning well and the tackling was sharp. Bell City had to punt only once early in the game and was never in trouble during the second half."

"Creole scored to lead 6-0 but Sonny Arceneaux scored to give Bell City the lead 7-6. A 52 yard Arceneaux pass set up a Broussard scoring lateral. Arceneaux to Miller extra point made it 14-6. As the half ended, an Arceneaux to Miller pass set up an Arceneaux score."

"Broussard's running and blocking set up 55 and 42 yard scoring romps by Arceneaux for Bell City to lead 33-19 in the third quarter. Fontenot, Fruge and Broussard set up 35 yard and 45 yard scores by Arceneaux as Bell City won by the final of 45-25."

In case you lost track of the scoring, that was six touchdowns for Sonny.

Arceneaux lays claim to another distinction. In the 1952-53 season, Bell City opened their schedule with a game against Grand Chenier. Sonny returned the first kick-off of the season back for a touchdown. The last game of the season was against Hackberry. In fact, the cheer at that game was "We want to know, we want to know, can you stop, Arceneaux?" Well, Hackberry couldn't stop Arceneaux on the opening kickoff, which he returned for a score. That's two opening kick-off returns in the first and last day of the season in which Bell City ended with a 6-2 record.

The Creole Pirates were coached by J.C. Reina, who recalls a scary incident that happened at practice one day.

One of the boys came out of a tackle with blood on his face. It seemed to be coming form his mouth. Coach Reina thought that maybe the boy had broken his lip or nose.

Coach takes up the story.

"Come to find out that his tongue was half completely hanging off and it really scared the heck out of me. We were a long way from any medical facilities. I knew there was a local doctor and I brought him there as quick as I could. He stuffed his mouth full of gauze and cotton to keep him from bleeding and told me to take him to Lake Charles."

Coach Reina loaded the boy in his old car and took him to the Lake Charles' St. Patrick's hospital. It seemed a long and tense drive.

"When I got there, they calmed my nerves. They said, 'It's a bad cut but it will be all right because the tongue is the flesh that heals very fast.' Sure enough, three days later he was out there wanting to play. But I didn't let him play for a few more days," says the coach.

Coach Reina was an inspiration to his players, too, like so many of the coaches. But sometimes, the head guy ran out of inspiration.

Coach recalls a game when his young Pirates had played in mud, were exhausted, given their all, and were losing. The team came to the sidelines for help.

"They looked to me for some inspiration. They saw me as some kind of God. But there just wasn't anything more I could do," recalls Coach Reina. "I'll never forget the helplessness I felt."

If the six-man coaches of the day couldn't always come up with the right words, overall they performed a special magic that transformed many of the young men they mentored.

Back in Bell City, Coach Theriot, for example, was mentoring, coaching and caring for his players. Arceneaux was made a captain in both his junior and senior years but the coach's impact was felt well beyond the football field.

"Clarence had a great influence on my life," says Sonny.

---

The Basile Bearcats 1950 State champions

Norbert Young
J.M. Gaspard
Sammy Essmeier
Orville Ardoin
Harold Christ, C.H. Doga
Charles Essmeier
Irvin Trahan
Chester Manuel
Louis Jeans
John Young
Lysses "Chick"Grainger

Ernest Duplechin
Lincoln Chapman
Rogers Aguillard (manager)
Eugene Hutson
John Bellon
Bobby Courtney
John Allen DeBarge
Linwood Guidry
Silton Aucoin
George Duhon
Stanford Johnson

Bell City Bear Cubs  1952-53

Sonny Arceneaux
Bradley Broussard
Curtis Fontenot
Everett Fusilier
Daryl Todd
Junior Miller
Norman Fruge
Benny Broussard
L.J. Primeaux
Algae Breaux
Earl Daughenbaugh
Harold Fusilier
Jesse Duhon
Herman Theriot
Buddy Broussard

Former players of Coach Lou Hanson celebrating his memorial day.

Coach Lou Hanson and Hanson Field

Bell City 1954 team. Top, left to right: Junior Miller, Sonny Arceneaux, Curtis Fontenot, Bradley Broussard, Jules Logncion, Daryl Todd, Earl Daughenbaugh, Norman Fruge, Coach Theriot. Middle: E. Gaspard, Willfred Istre, Pat Deroven, H. Fuselier, Benny Broussard, J. Clement, Jesse Duhon. Bottom: L. Sonnier, A. Breaux, L.J. Primeaux, R. Nunez, J. Fruge, J. Delaney.

# Broken Noses, a Frozen Sophomore, and a Two-Year Winning Streak

## Golden Meadow Lions and Larose Cut Off Bulldogs

What do Cut Off, Golden Meadow and Larose have in common? Unlikely as it seems, they were all football teams, who along with Lockport and Holy Savior introduced high school six-man football to Lafourche Parish in southern Louisiana in 1948. Other schools in the area were already playing eleven-man but for these above-mentioned five schools it was the first journey into football. And they played for six glorious seasons, creating athletes, excitement, and memories.

I have fond memories myself of this part of the Bayou and Cajun country. I coached football at Nicholls State University which is situated there, and loved every moment of my time amongst these great people.

Easton Pitre, who later became superintendent of this very same Lafourche District, recounts many great stories of both six-man and the times in which he grew up, in his book, "My World Was Wonderful."

At the end of the summer of 1948, Easton remembers a significant event that would change the lives of many. Some of the boys in the school were summoned to a meeting with the Principal, Mr. Miller, and a Math teacher, Mr. Rolufs.

"They announced the good news: Golden Meadow High School was going to field a football team. This was indeed fantastic news. No one in our school had ever played football before, including Mr. Rolufs, as our coach, and Mr. Miller his assistant. Mr. Miller was a 'born athlete' but had no football opportunities. We were eager."

Golden Meadow was starting from scratch. They practiced for a few days and then received their equipment, such as it was.

"No-one knew how to dress with all the pads handed out. The helmet was made out of leather-type material with no bars for face protection. "

During his two years on the six-man team Pitre broke his nose twice. There was no medical attention available.

"For a broken nose, one continued to play," writes Pitre.

The team had khaki pants used for both practice and games.

"The school splurged because we did have game jerseys, red or maroon in color. Our shoes were high tops with long cleats," says Pitre

Pitre, along with quarterback Allen Rebstock and tailback Linton Doucet, composed the offensive backfield and they played defense, too.

Apart from practicing in the summer heat, the tactical preparation was pretty informal.

The week before the opening game, quarterback Allen Rebstock told his coach that they didn't have any plays where he actually carried the ball, which wasn't taking advantage of his speed.

Coach Rolufs responded, "I didn't make the rules but if you come up with an acceptable play, we'll try it."

Rebstock did come up with a play and it worked all year for Golden Meadow. Easton Pitre describes it in his book.

"Allen (Rebstock) would get the snap, pitch to me at fullback. As I was moving straight up, I gave the ball to Linton (Doucet). Allen came around him and received the ball from Linton, but the opposite way from him. Allen would follow my blocking while Linton was going in the other direction. It worked all season. That success was due to the fact that Linton was a speedy runner, and defenses respected him. Really, Allen was a gifted runner, and he had the speed to beat defenses. It was especially true if the defense was slightly out of position because of the reverse effect."

It was soon time for the first football game in Golden Meadow history. Their opponents, Cut Off had already lost a close game to Lockport.

The stands were full. The opening kick-off of the Golden Meadow football era was memorable.

It didn't happen.

Easton Pitre explains.

"Allen was our kicker. He was more excited than any of us. Allen ran to the ball. Boom!!! Everybody was running to their coached position. Where is the ball? It is still on the tee. In his excitement, Allen had completely missed the ball."

Since he hadn't touched the ball no penalty was awarded and the kicker given another chance. The whistle blew a second time.

"Boom!!! Everyone ran to his coached position. Where's the ball? Is it still on the tee? No, it fell off with the wind velocity caused by Allen's foot when he missed again."

The referee, sparing the young man's blushes, simply gave the ball to Cut Off on their own 35 yard line.

But Rebstock made up for his missed kicks by scoring three times on the 2-3-1 reverse play he designed, and Golden Meadow led 33-0 at halftime,which was the final score.

"After the game, all of us (Cut Off players included) were overflowing with joy. We had played the first football game in our area."

Pitre especially remembers one play.

"On one of Allen's touchdown runs, he passed me up and realizing he was unchallenged in his run, I slowed down to a jog. Bam!! Someone hit me with a body block, and sent me down tumbling. After the game I asked one of the Terrebonne twins why he had thrown a block on me when it didn't mean anything. He replied, 'It was too tempting. You were an easy target.' He weighed only about one hundred and forty to my two hundred."

Next week, there was a rematch with Cut Off on home soil. Home soil was actually a softball field with grass that was two feet high in some places, appropriate for a school called Golden Meadow, but not conducive to athletic competition. The players cut the grass during the week, with plenty of local help. The school board sent in some bleachers.

Golden Meadow racked up the wins. They were 5-0 until they played Holy Savior and were shredded by a runner called Edmond Becnel. But Golden Meadow won the return visit. The final game of the season was played at Larose on a very cold night and blankets were the only things to keep the players warm.

"When the score reached 48-0 in Golden Meadow's favor, coach started sending in all the younger players who hadn't had much, or any, chance to play during the season thus far. Not all of them were excited at the opportunity."

Pitre writes that sophomore Harrison Cheramie refused. "He told the coaches it was too cold and he wasn't surrendering that blanket."

This pragmatic view of the world was later in evidence when Harrison became a respected community leader.

The regular season was over and Golden Meadow had a terrific 7-1 record. But there was one game left.

"The Larose VFW had decided to sponsor the LHSAA's Bydistrict game with a bowl game, the Oyster Bowl. We would be the host team. Our opponents would be the Buras High Wildcats."

Buras had been playing six-man for a few years and were undefeated, a record they maintained with a 31-6 win.

Larose Cut Off have a tremendous history in six-man. Their story has a lot to do with the oil boom that reshaped the area in the early 1950s. Larose and Cutoff had been two separate schools but were consolidated into Larose Cut Off High School (LCO) in 1950 to better accommodate the surging communities.

The use of tractors and other mechanization also changed the landscape, literally and metaphorically. One consequence was that children weren't needed as much to work in the fields thus allowing them to stay in school longer.

Coach Roland Chiasson had the opportunity to build an athletics program from scratch when he took over at LCO.

"There was no program so I had the opportunity to begin a program with football, baseball, basketball and track."

The Coach developed an impressive team. Though the Bulldogs lost their first game in the 1951 season, they won all of the remainder of their games. It was a streak the coach wanted to keep going the following season.

"I didn't talk about winning a state championship. I did this because we started a winning streak the year before. I felt in fairness to other kids we wanted to try to continue that winning streak. So we concentrated on game to game, just win one game at a time, and forget about the state championship. We erased it from our minds. We just wanted to continue winning games."

Coach Chiasson was incredibly successful using this philosophy.

"It so happened that we won that year and we did the same thing the next year to continue the winning  streak. But the championship game was furthest from our minds until we finally got into the playoffs."

Shaeffer Curole, who played offensive and defensive end says, "Coach Chiasson could have gone into any town, any city in the United States, picked up fourteen individuals, get them in shape, teach the game like he did, and he'd have won a state championship."

Irvin Adams, teacher and assistant coach says, "I think a lot had to do with his personality. You do it right. If you do it wrong, you learn how to do it right. That was his attitude. I'm sure his discipline had a lot of carryover from his time in the Marines."

His time in the Marines. Coach Roland Chiasson had, in fact, won the Silver Star in the performance of his Marine duties.

Philip Collins recalls the equipment was old and worn and "Coach Chiasson had to repair most of the shoulder and hip pads himself."

Quarterback Sidney Triche remembers that the pads were ill-fitting, had no foam protection and actually slowed the players down.

"They didn't have the foam that they have today so it cut down your speed quite a lot. Everything was taped up because it was so loose."

Collins recalls a game against Woodland where the opponents came out in brand spanking new blue and white uniforms and "fancy helmets". It seemed like Woodland had a full roster.

Collins recalls, "There might have been forty guys all lined up coming on that field and here we are in old scraggly uniforms with pants held up by tape."

It didn't take long for LCO to take charge, however. It was quickly 21-0, then 40-0. Would there be any mercy?

Coach Chiasson recalls, "There was a rule that said when there was a 45-point difference, the game was over. I went to their coach and he wanted to stop it. I wanted to stop the game. But I learned that the officials had to agree to it. Now, I don't know why the officials kept the game going. I'm still wondering about that today."

A newspaper report of the game stated:

"The Larose Cut Off Bulldogs slaughtered a game, but outmanned and lighter Woodlawn six-man team 96-0 on a muddy field at Woodlawn High, Friday September 19."

"Every possible player and combination was used defensively and offensively by Coach Roland Chaisson, but the score kept mounting as every combination clicked."

An editorial at the time blasted the refs.

"We might point out that there is a definite rule in the book that says a game is to be stopped any time one team gets 45 points ahead at the beginning of or during the second-half. This rule was not enforced in LCO's first two contests away from home. Such indicates poor officiating and should not be allowed to happen in Lafourche Parish. When one team is that far ahead it ceases to be a contest anyway."

The officials must have taken notice. Here's a newspaper report of a game played shortly after.

"Scoring a touchdown 35 seconds after the opening kick-off, the powerful Larose Cut Off Bulldogs went on from there and defeated a hard-trying Holy Savior High six-man outfit 48-0, in a game that only lasted 24 playing minutes."

"The contest on the Holy Savior gridiron at Lockport Sunday was automatically stopped at the half because of the rule which ends six-man games whenever one team is ahead by 45 points at, or after the half."

The Bulldogs were in midst of a remarkable 28 game winning streak in which they shut out their opponents nine times.

This streak took them to a critical 1952 game against Buras, the only team to have beaten them in two seasons.

A preview of the "championship" in the local paper read like this.

"Buras won the state championship last year and appears to be just as strong this season. LCO lost to Buras by some four TDs in its opener in 1951, and the Bulldogs are determined to avenge that defeat Sunday."

"Both teams are undefeated. In fact, neither has even been crowded this season. With proper enforcement of the 45-point-lead rule the Bulldogs would not have gotten to finish a single game. The last two contests were halted at halftime."

The newspaper headlined this as the "championship game" but admitted that while the statement "was not technically true, we're convinced that the winner of the scrap will go on to win the title."

The account of this critical game read like this.

"The aggressive Larose Cut Off Bulldogs defeated their greatest opposition by smashing the Buras Wildcats by 26-6."

Larose Cut Off jumped out to a quick lead. On his own 25, Philip Collins, "started around end, reversed his field and smashed his way to a tally."

After LCO's Jimmy David intercepted a pass in the end zone, the quarterback David then connected with Jake Guidry on a 17-yard scoring pass. Numa Breaux then scored on fourth and goal from the one. Guidry scored again on a 12-yard pass from Sidney Triche to make it 26-0 at halftime.

Larose Cut Off did make it to the state championship against McKowen.

Here's the account.

"Undefeated Larose Cut Off won the Southeast district six-man football championship tonight, coming from behind to score a lopsided 43 to 10 triumph over McKowen High of Jackson."

"Phillip Collins, Bobby Pierce and Melvin Guidroz carried the winners to their 17th consecutive triumph over a two-season period. Collins scored four touchdowns, Pierce notched two and Guidroz tallied one touchdown and caught a pass for an extra point."

"We took it all in our stride. It didn't go to the community's heads because we won the championship. I think that carried over because we won the Class A championship in 1966 and then we won another championship, around 1974," said Coach Chaisson in an interview recorded before his death in 2008.

"They didn't get swell-headed over it. Teamwork, learning your plays, knowing every play. we'd practice for hours. We had over a hundred plays and every one had to be done to perfection in practice," said Chaisson.

---------------

Larose Cut Off 1952 State champions

Loyman Melancon
Kernest Pierce
Albert Savoie
Sidney Triche
Melvin Guidroz
Numa Breaux
Shaeffer Curole
Bobby Pierce
Jimmy David
Jake Guidry
Phillip Collins

Golden Meadow six-man team 1948

Larose Cut Off 1952 State Champions. Top from left: George Hebert, Assistant
Coach; Jimmy David, Phillip Collins, Shaeffer Curole, Jake Guidry, Numa
Breaux, Bobby Pierce, Sidney Triche, Clyde Acosta, Roland Chaisson, Coach.
Bottom: Felix Guidroz, Loyman Melancon, Albert Savoie, Melvin Guidroz,
Kernest Pierce, Ray Savoie, Manager.

# Speed, Lost Teeth, and the Homecoming Queen

## Livonia Wildcats and Morganza Tigers

Livonia High School is in Pointe Coupee Parish, an area with a proud tradition in six-man and eight-man football. Livonia won the six-man title in 1956 and then in consecutive years in 1962 and 1963. They then switched to eight-man and won championships in 1964 and 1965, making four successive years of championship football. Their rivals, Morganza, won the six-man championship in 1955.

As you can read elsewhere in this book (see the chapter on the Refs), Livonia supporters could be a passionate and unrelenting crowd and not just on the sports field. The Livonia High School was scheduled to be closed in the early nineties but parent protests prevented the closure. On the other hand, Morganza School was closed and is currently used by the Pointe Coupee Sheriff's Office as a training facility.

Let's begin with Morganza's 1955 championship game. The Tigers had some fast runners. Joe Guidroz who played on the Livonia 1956 championship team remembers.

"We had a lot of fast people in Pointe Coupee Parish. I'll give you an example: Bobby Fanning. The national record for the hundred-yard dash was 9.2 and he could run a 9.4. He ran for Southeastern. And they had a couple more guys that could break 9.8, 9.7 on that Morganza team."

Ignatius "Hucky" Purpera, the quarterback and Clarence "Woots" Wells, a lineman were first team all-state players and along with Fanning and Herbie Plauche, led the 1955 Tigers to the title game. Their opponents were the tough Creole Pirates and the game was played on Friday, December 2, 1955, under the lights at a rain-soaked Immaculate Conception field at Chenal.

The Pirates took the opening kick-off and scored on their first drive when Earl Roberts got to the outside and scored on a twenty-yard run. It didn't take long for the Tigers to reply.

Larry Porche, writing for the Pointe Coupee Banner, described it like this.

"The Pirates kicked and Winfield LeBlanc returned it to the 26 yard line. Little Pat Donovan drove through center for eighteen yards. On the next play, Steve Landry, following excellent blocking, went to the fifteen yard line. The next play, Steve again swept around the end for the first Tiger tally. Herb Plauche went round end for the only extra point made in the ball game for either team. Score: 7-6."

The weather made handling the ball difficult and there were numerous fumbles. This made the game an uncharacteristically defensive one for six-man. Both teams punted on consecutive possessions in the second quarter. Then, Creole surprised the Tigers when quarterback Fred Nunez threw to the aptly named Robert Mudd, who was downed at the Tigers ten-yard line. The Pirates fumbled on the Tiger three- yard line and Morganza's Gene Ransome recovered. The Tigers couldn't advance and on their next drive Creole scored when Nunez threw to Roberts to make the score 12-7.

"After the Pirates kicked, the mighty Tigers began to show their superiority by crashing through the line for long gains. The drive was climaxed with Herb Plauche fighting his way for thirty yards and the second Tiger TD," wrote Larry Porche.

Morganza received the second half kick-off and in five plays they had marched to the Pirate's one yard line. They were penalized five yards on the next play, however, their only penalty of the game.

140

"The next play proved fatal for the Pirates," wrote Porche. "Hucky Purpera hit Gene Ransome in the end zone with a beautiful pass for the final touchdown."

Morganza had their championship but it didn't take long for Livonia to claim theirs.

Livonia's program had humble beginnings. Gerald Hawkins, member of the 1956 team recalls, "The coach would give us a little talk, and we'd load up on the bus, and we'd go to the game. Most of the time we played on a Sunday afternoon. Nobody had lights and a lot of schools didn't even have their own fields. So, we'd play on a community field or a neutral field somewhere."

The coach didn't know too much about football. According to Hawkins, "The head coach was a math teacher at school. He had no football experience. We designed our own plays and our captain, Tommy Bergeron, who was our right end, called all the plays during the game."

Hawkins remembers Bergeron as a tough leader who would do what ever it took to win.

"I remember that sometimes when we had a running back that we had trouble with, Tommy would ask to get in and play a little defense. I recall Rougon had a running back who was tromping all over us one day, and Tommy says, "Put me in, Coach. I'll stop him." And he busted his helmet on him, and it was a plastic helmet. And the running back for Rougon woke up in St. Joseph Hospital in New Roads."

But Livonia had some tough running backs of their own. Dan Cowen is remembered as an uncompromising runner. Orville Durham who moved to the area in time to play on the 1956 team remembers Dan Cowen as a "big, old boy, but he was a fullback. Dan Cowen would run over you. We considered him a monster. He weighed about 185 or 190 pounds. That was big, then."

Durham, whose dad was a pipe fitter, had a transient childhood having attended no fewer than 17 high schools. He had played eleven- man in Nebraska and Texas before landing at Livonia. His first glimpse of six-man was a surprise.

"When I arrived on site at Livonia, I looked around and I couldn't believe it. It didn't look like they had anybody on the field. It looked like they had one team on the field. And I had never seen that before."

Durham remembers another runningback on the Livonia team.

"Vic Bellelo was a good friend of mine. He could run. He'd run right at you, and you didn't want to tackle him when he's running right at you because his knees would knock all your teeth out. They'd come up to about his chin when he was running."

Dental care was an ever present concern when tackling or carrying the ball in six-man. Not that Dave Cowen worried about such small matters.

Joe Guidroz remembers an incident involving the uncompromising Cowen.

"We were practicing one day. He got all his front teeth knocked out, and he took his teeth and he went and put them by the goal post so he could find them later. Then, he kept practicing like nothing ever happened! His mouth was bleeding and he just kept right on. I think he picked up his teeth at the end of practice and took them home with him."

Guidroz was a second team all-state selection. He was occasionally critical of his coach because he was really a math teacher not a football expert.

Guidroz says, "Our coach didn't know much football, and I used to be critical of him because he didn't know much. But I remember talking to one of my fellow players, Danny Aucoin, who reminded me that if that coach hadn't taken us, we wouldn't have had a team. Nobody else would coach us. So, now I think back, I should have been grateful to coach and not critical. Pointe Coupee Parish didn't pay their coaches very well, and I think he did it because he cared about us."

That level of caring led to all manner of relationships. Linda Carrier Walker graduated from Livonia in 1957. As a cheerleader, she had enthusiastically supported the six-man team, especially through their championship season.

"I cherish that memory, and I cherish all these guys that I graduated with, most of those guys that finished from the '56 championship team. So, we had a good time, and it was a lot of great memories."

1956 was a special year for Linda, too. She was named as Livonia's first homecoming queen. And that championship team would leave a lasting impression on Linda's life.

She became friends with one of those players, Jimmy Walker.

"Jimmy is a year younger than I am, so we didn't really get together until after we got out of school, and we started dating later. I was working in Baton Rouge and everything. So, we got together again, and we married and have four children, nine grandchildren, and one great grandchild. So, we've had a good life and a lot of good memories."

And those folks who were around in Pointe Coupee Parish have a lot of fond memories of their championship football teams.

---

Morganza 1955 State championship team

Coach Luther Robillard
Assistant Coach P.J. Guedry
Lawrence Crochet
Winfield LeBlanc
Johnny LeCoq
Gene Ransome
Donald Witty

Clarence "Woots" Wells
Winfield LeCoq
L.J. Guedry
Nolan LeCoq
Pat Donovan
Steve Landry
Ignatius "Hucky" Purpera
Wallace Vosburg
Herb Plauche
Bobby Fanning
John Allen Landry

Livonia High School 1956 State Champions. Top, from left: Dan Keowan, Jack Jones, Johnny Newton, J.A. Chenevert, Pat Bearry, Gerald Faveron, Alvin Brown, Orval Durham, Johnny Walker, Coach Kelly Goudeau, Trainer Clarence Thibodeaux. Bottom: Danny Aucoin, Charles LeBlanc, Paul Poche, James Scallan, Neil Smith, Jimmy Walker, Richard Morgan, Robert Soulier, Charles Pinsonat, Ray LeJeune

1955 Morganza team. Top, from left: Lawrence Crochet, Winfield LeBlanc, Johnny LeCoq, Gene Ransome, John Allen Landry, Donald Witt, Clarence "Woots" Wells, Winfield LeCoq. Bottom: L.J. Guidry, Nolan LeCoq, Jerrold Purpera, Pat Donovan, Steve Landry, Hucky Purpera, Wallace Vosburg, Herb Plauche, Bobby Fanning.

# Stepping In, Stepping Over, Stepping Up[1]

## Rayne High School Wolves

Six-man football started at Rayne in 1941. Braxton (B.I.) Moody, a business legend in these parts, wrote in his memoir *A Boy from Iota* that in his senior year he played six-man "because most of the other boys were drafted or had enlisted in the various branches of the armed services and we didn't have enough boys to play eleven-man."

The 1941 Rayne team, according to Moody, "weren't that good but did win as many games as we lost." Their starting team consisted of Herbert Hernandez, Will Robert Kennedy, Charles 'Moon' Chappuis, Roy Derise, Clyde Melancon and Braxton Moody.

Moody was called "Grapevine" because he was "tall and slender, 6'4" and weighed 165 pounds". He writes, "I could catch a pass anywhere within ten yards of me. I was also the team punter. I made more touchdowns than anyone else."

And then Moody and his buddies graduated.

History lifted them from the peaceful, joyful charm of their adolescence on the Bayou and instantly transported them to a traumatized adulthood on the war-torn battlefields of Europe and the treacherous terrain of the Japanese islands.

---

[1] I am indebted to **Mr, Charles Sidney Stutes, The Rayne Tribune and The Crowley Daily Signal for their information and stories which were the foundation of this chapter. Braxton Moody and Tommy Petitjean also contributed.**

The senior students and teachers of the Greatest Generation left a huge gap when they answered the call. And the call of duty was noticeable everywhere including Rayne High School in 1944. The Coach, Vincent Chappius and the Principal, William Sonnier, were in the service, as were many others. In fact, there was only one male member of the faculty, George H. Johnson, as the 1944 school year started.

Rayne is in Acadia parish and has an area of less than four square miles. It is known as the 'frog capital of the world' a theme which was started when a gourmet chef introduced the delicacy in the 1880s. The frog theme has proved riveting. As many as 50,000 frog legs were shipped out at a time and the frog tradition thrived and grew.

Irene Petitjean, the first female Principal in Acadia Parish, had been in charge since 1942. She stepped in when the men stepped out and was to play an integral part in the story of the 1944 Rayne Wolves season.

When the Wolves played their first game, there was little indication of the things to come. Rayne had a young team, largely because many of the older boys were at war. J. B. Sheperd at 17 was the oldest member of the team. Tommy Petitjean, a promising sophomore quarterback, was just 14, and four others; Louis Morvant, Willie Lognion, Vincent Dupuis and Deleon Trahan were freshmen.

On Friday, October 6th at just before 3pm, the Rayne boys started their season on their home field. It was a home field that the players themselves prepared. Tommy Petitjean recalls that, "we made our own field, cut our own grass, marked it off for games."

As the game was about to start, two armed trucks carrying about a dozen German POWs was seen coming up Polk Street, a reminder of the context of the times. There were about 200 prisoners held at Gossen Park Prisoners Camp just two blocks away, and this group was about to help harvest the rice crop.

The visiting Jeanerette Tigers were the reigning state champions, a tough and experienced team who took no prisoners. Jeanerette had already won their first game of the season and were going to prove a difficult challenge for the young Rayne team. Indeed, Jeanerette jumped out to a 13-0 lead. On the kick-off after the Tigers second touchdown, the 16 year-old Buddy Gilbert took the kick and ran the ball all the way back for his first ever touchdown. It was the first of many.

Despite holding the Tigers to just one more score, Rayne fell 20-7. Coach Johnson, the only male on the faculty, was "well-pleased with the fine showing of the Wolves."

Legendary coach Vince Lombardi is credited with saying, "Winning isn't everything, it's the only thing." The quote has often been misinterpreted as meaning that coach Lombardi was only interested in the score at the end of the game. Far from it. Lombardi's own writings, as well as testimony of former players, attest to the fact that what Lombardi meant was that preparing oneself in every way, mentally and physically, for the challenge ahead is what really mattered. Striving to win and the dedication to that goal was the key, not necessarily the scoreboard at the end of the game. The Rayne boys had given their all and it inspired an incredible response.

When Lombardi was a basketball coach at Fordham (yes, he really was!), he made his players physically cross the end line every day in practice as a symbolic commitment of the pursuit of total dedication.

Several people were about to similarly step over that line at Rayne.

Principal Irene was a busy lady. She could have just been satisfied with the boys' efforts against Jeanerette. She didn't just settle, however. She stepped up. She was incredibly enthusiastic in her support for the team. She couldn't give the boys enough praise. She was at once their biggest cheerleader. Motivated by their Principal's excitement, four more boys stepped over the line and joined the team.

And then someone else stepped over and up.

Lee Mayeux was an interesting local figure. He owned a Purina Feed store in town that had a bright checkerboard storefront. Mayeux was quite the local personality, smart, personable, even bold. Mayeux had been a football star at SLI and now helped the game he loved by refereeing local games. Like the one between Rayne and Jeanerette.

If truth be told, George Johnson, the male faculty, wasn't really a football coach. His passion was basketball and he would later become a Louisiana basketball coaching legend and Principal. As Mayeux refereed that first game, he could see that Johnson was really a novice. But he could also see that the boys were talented and committed. Shortly after the game, Mayeux offered his services. He would help Coach Johnson with the Rayne Wolves six-man football team.

Mayeux and Johnson worked on some adjustments in the week following that first game against Jeanerette. Mayeux would ultimately help in a practical way by getting new uniforms through his connection with Professor Wilbacks at his alma mater, SLI. But that would be the least of his contributions. For now, the Wolves stuck with the kit they had got when Adolph Sommer donated a war bond for raffle before the season's start. The money thus collected went to buy the uniforms.

Uniforms were an unregulated commodity at this time. Some had numbers, some didn't. They came in different shapes and styles. St. Martinsville came up with a particularly clever wrinkle that took action by the governing Louisiana Athletic Association to eventually iron out.

The mothers of the St. Martinsville team had sewn leather-like material in the shape of a football into the front of the team jerseys. In the heat of the action it was very difficult for opponents to distinguish this insert from the real ball! St. Martinsville ran up some huge scores before the Association outlawed the kit.

Rayne's second game, also at home, was against another tough opponent, Assumption of the Immaculate Conception (AIC) from Opelousas in St. Landry Parish. AIC featured all-state halfback Ben Perry and a host of outstanding players. It was played on Friday, October 13, and as the date suggests, it was an auspicious moment that had portents for the future.

Buddy Gilbert ran four yards for the first touchdown and then completed a long pass to Buddy Moody for a second score before Perry's running led to an unconverted touchdown. On the ensuing kick-off, however, Gilbert ran the ball all the way back for the score to give Rayne a 20-6 halftime lead.

In the second half, AIC's Perry took over, leading to a score that made it 20-13 and another drive that took them to the Rayne two-yard line. Now, remember that a goal-line stand was a tough thing to make in six-man. There were many more wide open spaces than in eleven-man. Gaining two yards in six-man would be like gaining six inches in eleven-man.

The Rayne defense stiffened. They stopped them on first and second down. A heroic tackle stopped the third down play short of the goal line. Then the unthinkable – they stopped them on fourth down, too! Petitjean, the 14 year-old quarterback and cousin of the Principal, fifteen year-old Rodney Hoffpauir and 16 year-old Maxie Navarre, were singled out in reports for their fine defensive efforts. Petitjean and Navarre both had interceptions and Bobby Craig had two. But Craig wasn't finished.

Taking over virtually on their own goal line, Rayne marched down the field. When Bobby Craig caught a touchdown pass from Buddy Gilbert, it sealed a fantastic 27-13 win. The Rayne Wolves were on their way.

Getting on your way anywhere was a problem everywhere in 1944, including Louisiana. Rationing and self-sacrifice were still the order of the day. There were checks on the quality of your tires. Gas coupons limited travel to ninety miles of personal driving a month. All service stations were closed on a Sunday but one was kept open on a rotating basis in case of emergencies. No phones were installed in Rayne after 1942 and users were encouraged to keep calls short.

All of this presented a problem for both players and fans trying to get to a road game. Bus transfers could not be used for something as inessential as a football game. The Rayne community once again stepped up. Meeting at Bobby Craig's house across from the school, parents brought their cars. Typically, one would have enough gas coupons but badly worn tires. The solution: Rotate roadworthy tires from one car to another, so cars with enough gas coupons also had good tires. Thus, the tire exchange system was born.

Players and fans were thus transported to the Lake Arthur School on that last Friday in October as Rayne took on the Tigers. Everyone got to play, even the second string, as the Wolves, led by Gilbert's four touchdowns and Moody's three, won 46-27.

The win energized Rayne's self-belief and it fueled their next effort, an away game at tough St. Peter's.

When players and fans showed up for a night game against powerhouse St Peters of New Iberia that last Friday in October, they saw a tremendous source of energy near the sidelines. No, it wasn't the coach or the cheerleaders. It was a pile of coal for the school's furnace. But closer inspection also found lumps of coal all over the field. Undeterred by presence of these coal deposits, Rayne smoked the home team. Gilbert had another three touchdowns and again everybody got to play. One journalist wrote, "The Wolves ran roughshod over St Peter's who couldn't cope with the Gilbert-Moody combination." Final score: Rayne 58 St Peters 18.

After a bye week courtesy of a scheduling error, Rayne was slated to host the Sacred Heart Trojans on Friday November, 10th. This was a very special day. It was the first homecoming in Rayne's history.

The Principal Miss Irene was in charge of the festivities and the identity of the homecoming queen would remain secret until she was crowned by the captain of the football team, Bobby Craig, at halftime.

The town was abuzz as Homecoming day dawned in beautiful weather. At school, excitement was in the air, studies were not. The school was decorated in its purple and gold colors with Red, White and Blue to celebrate Armistice Day. That's Armistice Day to commemorate the end of World War I. No one was sure when that day, commemorating the end of World War II would come, but it was nearer than most dared to hope, but still not soon enough for some.

Paula Stamm, Kathleen McBride, Rita Sonnier, Agnes Gueno, and Anna Marie Butcher were cheerleaders and not long after the clock struck noon, they led a pep rally in Depot Square. Shortly thereafter, when the cheerleaders were pinned with corsages, "the largest crowd ever in Rayne High School history," gathered to witness the fifth game of the Wolves' season.

In anticipation of such a large crowd, bleachers had been brought in from South Rayne's Ricebird baseball stadium. Not long afterwards, some adventurous young students looking for some excitement, decided to bet amongst themselves on the sturdiness of the new bleachers. Those who bet that the bleachers would collapse when subjected to excessive force, won. The rickety, wooden edifice was no match for adolescent exuberance and duly collapsed in surrender.

Miss Irene, who certainly wasn't one to surrender, promised to withhold diplomas until the school was compensated. But that was a long way in the future. There was a game to play. And it was, as usual, played with spectators standing on the sidelines.

The Trojans were a big, strong team but, according to written reports, "folded under a barrage of passes from Buddy Gilbert." Moody caught two touchdowns, Craig, Navarre and Petitjean one each. Navarre also recovered a fumble for a touchdown and Gilbert ran a punt back fifty yards and a kick-off back seventy yards for touchdowns. Final score: Rayne 54 Sacred Heart 21.

The Homecoming Queen Rita Sonnier and her court Dolores Irion, Betty Jane Bernard, Geraldine Kennedy, Wanda Burrow and Lois Trahan, were hosts in the home of Mrs. Willie Sonnier, whose husband had just been promoted to captain in the U.S. Army. Miss Irene insisted that Scared Heart's Reverend Irving DeBlanc, who is featured in their story in this book, be invited to the event, too.

Later, there was a dance at the South Rayne gym, which kicked off with the entrance of Captain Bobby Craig and Queen Rita Sonnier. The evening ended with everyone paying tribute to an honor roll list of Rayne High School boys at war. Those boys were serving on the battlefields of Europe when they should have been playing on the six-man fields of Louisiana.

The assembled guests sang an emotional version of God Bless America as their minds turned eastwards to missing friends, uncles, brothers, and fathers. Some of those Rayne boys never came home. Rodney Bergeron, Lawrence Bouillion, Lee Bruner, Edward Hoffpauir, Robert Hunter Woodrow LeBlanc, Earl Primeaux, Roy Schexneider and George Weil, gave the supreme sacrifice and will always be remembered.

But Rayne's football success was a great distraction from the events in Italy, France and across Europe. The town was distracted and captivated by their team's football success. The three Bs, Buddy Gilbert, Bobby Craig, and Buddy Moody, were getting noticed outside of Rayne. At North Rayne Central School, first graders viewed the high school boys with awe. Their Principal, Miss Bertha Kennedy, encouraged the Rayne boys to visit her school and called them "All-American."

But the season was only half over. There were serious challenges ahead and one loomed large. The visit of Cathedral – Carmel of Lafayette, who came to Rayne on the third Friday in November with only one loss and a lot of momentum. Rayne players and fans alike were warned that it would be a tough game.

The three Bs led Rayne to a 21-7 lead behind the "superior play-calling and blocking of Petitjean, Navarre and Hoffpauir."

Cathedral scored again to narrow the gap to 21-14 but Rayne answered. The teams then traded touchdowns like manic stock traders on Wall Street. Dramatic, spectacular plays were the norm. With less than two minutes to go, Rayne led 51-42. But Cathedral somehow contrived a score to pull within two.

The erudite and dramatic Miss Irene wrote, "It was like a dark, cold chill had suddenly descended from the heavens." And it was about to get chillier.

Cathedral ripped off a huge play and took the lead 55-51 with thirty seconds left.

Rayne had one last chance. Tommy Petitjean called all the plays. That was what Coach Mayeux demanded and Petitjean was in the huddle, ready to call a play that hopefully would get them a big chunk of the sixty yards they needed to win.

Many years later Petitjean recalled that moment.

"We were losing by a few points and in the last play of the game Bobby Craig, our center, called the play. I called the rest of the plays all year but he called that particular play."

Bobby said, "throw the ball to me." The plan was for Petitjean to lateral to Buddy Gilbert and for him to throw it downfield.

According to written reports, "Gilbert dropped back and heaved a long, mighty fifty yard pass into the arms of a wide open Craig – who ran the necessary ten yards for the touchdown."

Final score: Rayne 57, Cathedral 55.

The sun shone once again and ever brighter in Miss Irene's sky.

The Wolves played just five days later at Breaux Bridge, a newcomer to six-man football. The Wednesday afternoon game was in deference to the upcoming Thanksgiving weekend. Although it was Breaux Bridge's Homecoming the team probably should have stayed in school. Buddy Gilbert scored seven touchdowns as Rayne won 88-0.

Now, the only thing that seemingly stood in the way of a championship appearance for Rayne was a game against undefeated Gonzales.

But others had different ideas.

The Daily World newspaper in Opelousas argued that AIC should have a rematch with St. Peters for the championship. St. Peters had beaten them in the first game of the season and subsequently beaten powerhouse Sacred Heart. The paper conveniently forgot to mention the fact that both St. Peters and AIC had two losses (and both had lost to Rayne) and Rayne had only one. Still, AIC lobbied that there should be a rematch with St. Peters to determine the state championship.

Hearing the news, Miss Irene stepped up and over. She called the Principal of AIC, Father Marin, but he was one step ahead. A meeting at Shreveport of the Executive Council of the Louisiana Athletic Association on Saturday afternoon had already been arranged and would determine the championship game.

Miss Irene, vowing that "this will not happen," gathered every available gas coupon and drove to Shreveport with her coaches, Mayeux and Johnson. Once in the meeting, there was a heated exchange of views between Coach Mayeux and Father Marin before the Executive Council adjourned.

The Council emerged with a political decision. There would be two playoffs. St. Peters would play AIC and Rayne would play Gonzales. The winners would then, *presumably*, meet for the championship? As he left the meeting, Coach Mayeux apparently turned to the AIC contingent and said, "All right then, we'll just have to whoop you good."

Rayne's semifinal was to be played at a neutral site in Crowley, which had a field with stands and lights. Tickets -- adults 50c, school children 25c -- were on sale all week at local stores and were in high demand.

At game time, the temperature plummeted towards freezing. Which made Tommy Petitjean's observation of his opponents even more startling.

"We played at Crowley Memorial Stadium and Gonzales was there, all barefooted. That was during the war and you couldn't get shoes, so they went barefoot," recalls Tommy.

As for the game played on the frozen tundra – well, almost -- Navarre recovered a fumble for a touchdown and then Gilbert intercepted a pass and returned it seventy yards for a score. Gonzales scored from close in to make it 13-6 at half time.

The game was a tight defensive struggle through the third quarter but Petitjean turned the pivotal play as time was running down. He intercepted a pass and returned it for a score. After that, the floodgates opened and the Wolves scored four more touchdowns to win 46-6.

In Opelousas, the Daily World was preparing for the visit of St. Peters with their usual hubris. They had concluded that St. Peter's only threat was their passer Rene Patout. They were right. Behind Ben Perry's running, AIC won 43-8.

The paper was less accurate in its next edition on Sunday when it concluded that "AIC have their first championship football team."

Hearing that AIC had declared themselves champions, Miss Irene called Father Marin again. She learned of AICs version of events. AIC were Class B champions and Rayne Class A champions, according to Father Marin. Apparently, Miss Irene was in "fighting mood" when she called the Louisiana Athletic Association and reportedly used "her best Sorbonne language" in expressing her opinion of AIC's position.

Miss Irene won the day. The LAA agreed that there was "no such thing as classes" in six-man football and ordered a final play-off between AIC and Rayne. The game was scheduled at McNaspy Stadium on Friday, December 8.

The stage was set. Would Coach Mayeux be able to deliver on his promise to "whoop you good?" Would the Daily World's manipulation influence the game? Would Miss Irene even be able to watch?

Lee Mayeux stepped up again. This is when he contacted Professor Wilbacks at SLI to get better uniforms. Excitement crackled through the town in the build-up to the game. A record crowd of 1600 showed up at McNaspy stadium.

Rayne took the opening kick-off and promptly marched down the field to score. One of the three Bs, Buddy Moody, was injured on the drive but replacement Leroy Monte stepped up and scored with his first touch when he caught a pass from Buddy Gilbert.

"AIC was not on their usual game and Rayne smothered them with passes," the Daily World reported later.

Gilbert was his usual spectacular self. He was 23 for 30 and scored four times. Rayne was ahead at half-time 32-8, and romped to the championship with a 53-27 victory.

The players were celebrated, toasted and honored at many community events. A banquet was held and Professor Wilbanks presented the championship trophy to Bobby Craig. An engraved plate boldly asserted Rayne as "La. High School Athletic Association State Champions, Six-Man Football, 1944." The players' names were engraved.

Miss Irene gave each player small, golden footballs engraved with the player's name and the inscription "Champions 1944" and that included Rodney Trahan, J.B. Shepherd, Jack Gueno, Gardner Schexnyder, and Delton Trahan. The coaches were also celebrated.

SLI Athletic Director R.L Brown delivered an address in which he stressed the value of sports and how they shaped a boys life, "mentally, morally and physically."

Buddy Gilbert went off to join the Navy in 1945 but returned for his senior year and led the Wolves back into the championship game after another one-loss season. They lost in the title game to Sacred Heart by two points.

Tommy Petitjean got a scholarship to play at LSU, Buddy Gilbert went to SLI and Bobby Craig played at McNeese State.

But what about the boys of 1941, the ones who stepped in, stepped over and stepped up for a larger cause?

Herbert Hernandez joined the Marines and served in Iwo Jima and Saipan. On returning to the U.S., he earned a degree in education from LSU, taught history and became a Principal and Head Coach.

Will Robert Kennedy enlisted in the Army Air Corps, flew all across Asia in the war against Japan and became a crop-duster on his return.

Charles 'Moon' Chappuis, graduated from Officers Candidate School, and served as a platoon leader of a tank company in Germany. He eventually retired from the Army Reserves with rank of Major. He earned a law degree and served as a city attorney.

Roy Derise volunteered for the US Navy and was assigned to the USS Saratoga, which was hit by four bombs and three kamikaze pilots. Roy made it home and retired as a lab technician.

Clyde Melancon enlisted in the Marines and participated in three wars. His unit fought in Peleliu and New Caledonia and he also served in Korea and Vietnam. After thirty years he retired as Chief Master Sergeant. He worked as Vice President in Braxton Moody's business for ten years.

Braxton 'B.I.' Moody volunteered for duty with the Navy and was assigned to the USS Randolph, which attacked Iwo Jima and launched strikes against mainland Japan. He returned home, earned his CPA and became incredibly successful, hailed as "esteemed business genius" and philanthropist. The University of Louisiana-Lafayette, formerly SLI, named the Moody School of Business and Moody Hall in his honor

These men, and many like them, stepped in when they were needed. They stepped over that line every single day for their country. And when it was needed the most, they stepped up for freedom.

The 1944 "Starting Six." Top, left to right: Tommy Petitjean, Buddy Gilbert, Rodney Hoffpauir. Bottom: Maxie Navarre, Bobby Craig, Buddy Moody.

1944 "Wolf Reserves." Left to right: J.D. Monceaux, Jack Gueno, Rodney Trahan, Lenes Lavergne, Gardner Schexnyder, Conerly Estes, Leroy Monte.

# Underpaid, Abused, and Loving It

# The Refs

No athletic competition is possible without an officiating crew. The guys who officiated six-man football were community-minded locals with a love of athletics, a history of participation in sports and pretty good cardiovascular systems.

Typically, officiating crews consisted of initially three, then four, guys who would often travel to and from games together. They were dedicated men who usually had long careers as officials and progressed to refereeing eleven-man football as six-man became an ever distant memory.

For sure, these refs did it for the love of the game and as a contribution to the community. In the 1950s the pay for officiating a game was $10. Moreover, expenses weren't reimbursed, meaning the refs had to pay for their own transport to and from games.

Gerald Didier graduated from Catholic High School in 1950 where he was a standout athlete, especially in baseball. In fact, he was signed by the Dodger organization and played for six years in the minor leagues. In 1954 he was introduced to refereeing by his brother Clyde.

"In six-man, you got a good look at blocking, holding and clipping. It was a great experience for me when I later got into eleven-man," says Gerald who eventually spent 35 years officiating high school, and 25 years officiating college games.

The game was fast and you had to be in shape to keep up. Sometimes you had to be fast to escape the wrath of the crowd. Probably every official of that era had a story or two about being confronted by angry spectators. Gerald is no exception.

"My dad had six sons who were all into sports so he had attended many, many games. But he had never seen me officiate. So he decided to come with me one hot Sunday afternoon when I was officiating a game between Livonia and Brusly."

Both sets of fans had a reputation for being raucous and this game was no exception. Like many schools, Brusly had no bleachers, so people were standing several rows deep on the sideline. It was a high scoring game and the refs called two Livonia touchdowns back for clipping. At the end of the game the Livonia fans were mad and confronted the officiating crew.

"I remember some women with umbrellas. They had those umbrellas and they surrounded us in the middle of the field and they charged us. No police anywhere. No security. We made it out of there in one piece, though. It was the last game my dad came to see me officiate," recalls Didier.

Allen Buddy LeBlanc recalls a similar experience.

St. Gabriel had a reputation as a tough place to officiate.

"They'd throw everything at you if you dropped a flag and they cussed you out and raised all kind of cane," says LeBlanc recalling one particular incident in which St. Gabriel were penalized when they had first and goal at their opponent's two-yard line.

"They were going in to score and we called a penalty. Well, here come the beer bottles and the cussing and the raising cane. I told the Principal and the Coach that they had to control the crowd or we were going to stop the game and I was going to throw a flag if I had to. I penalized them," remembers Allen.

Unfortunately, the fans weren't in a very receptive mood and they kept up their abuse.

"They kept on doing it. So I threw another flag, penalized them again and moved the ball back another fifteen yards. They kept on going and I threw another flag, I picked up the ball and moved it back another 15 yards. This kept happening. When it got to their own two-yard line, they were facing first and 78. We had to get escorted back to Baton Rouge that night," says LeBlanc.

LeBlanc recalls that St. James was another tough place to ref. One time, before the game, school officials reassured him and his crew that they would be fine.

"Just get to midfield as soon as the game ends and we can assure you that you can get out of here without being shot," was the message. I'm sure those school officials only meant it as reassurance and not in any way as intimidation.

Buddy LeBlanc, who graduated from Catholic High School in 1951 was another baseball star turned six-man official, confirms that "there was a lot of controversy in a lot of the games."

Most of the time the controversy was over what the crowd saw as blown calls but sometimes blown calls just didn't get noticed by anybody.

Allen Buddy LeBlanc recalls officiating a game at Shady Grove. It was an extremely tight and low scoring game, a rarity in six-man.

"A Shady Grove player muffed a punt, and the ball went into the end zone. I called a touchdown and it was the only score of the game. On the way home it suddenly dawned on me that I had made a mistake. The ball should have come out to the twenty. The game should have ended 0-0. Not one of the other officials caught it. Neither coach caught the mistake, either."

Perhaps that was just as well.

Six-man football could be unpredictable, putting a ref in a bind.

There was always a *slaughter* or *mercy* rule in six-man where a game could be stopped if it was too one-sided after at least one half of the game had been played. The point differential varied at different times but was typically between 35 and 50 points.

Buddy LeBlanc recalls one such occasion in a game played at Brusly.

"I wanted to stop the game that night because when it got to 50, the mercy rule came into play. Brusly was down 49-0 at the half and were being badly outplayed. I wanted to stop it but the Brusly coach raised cane, so we let them play on. Well, Brusly came back strong and won the game like 72-64 or something like that. It was the most running I ever did on the football field."

The aerial game also caused problems for the refs. Buddy LeBlanc has memory of one particular game featuring St. James, who had a long unbeaten streak, playing St John of Plaquemine, who had a dismal won-loss record at the time. Naturally, the St. James home fans were disappointed that their team were unexpectedly losing and started throwing beer bottles.

"St. John's threw a pass on every down," recalls LeBlanc. And the St James' fans threw bottles on every down, too.

General Levy Dabadie is a military legend from New Roads, which itself sports a remarkable history.

The General graduated from St. Joseph's Academy in 1943 having played in the Southeastern Conference basketball tournament as well as baseball and 'sandlot' football. He recalls players of his era.

"Ted Glazer, who became a very successful farmer, was a great running back as was Joe Cashio. I remember Larry Roy the quarterback who became a Jesuit priest. Also Kevin and Richard Landry were small guys but great runners."

Dabadie went on to LSU and got a football scholarship and played with such legends as Y.A. Tittle, Ray Coates, Red Knight and Jim Cason.

Dabadie progressed to have a distinguished military career, which began as combat infantry to a glider regiment and service in Japan immediately after that country's surrender. He later served in the Louisiana National Guard becoming Commander of the 225th Engineer Brigade, Chief of Staff, Commander of Installations at Jackson Barracks in New Orleans, Camp Beauregard in Pineville and Camp Villere in Slidell.

The General loved sports and as his career was evolving, he became a six-man official. No doubt, his combat training and understanding of hostile forces stood him in good stead when refereeing.

"It was pretty tough. They had tough crowds and there wasn't a lot of security. And you had to be very, very careful because they'd come after you," recalls the General.

"They just wouldn't give up," said the General, and he wasn't just talking about the Japanese Imperial Marines that he and his fellow soldiers had to flush out of hiding as the war was coming to a conclusion.

"I remember one time we had to be escorted out of Livonia by the sheriff's department and the local police because Livonia had lost the game on a call we made against them. The fans were very irritated and upset," says the combat veteran.

Sometimes angry fans would execute a sneak attack.

The General recalls, "We officials all traveled together in the same car. One time we got to our car and all the tires were flat!"

Dabadie also recalls a very close game between Livonia and Morganza for the championship game around 1953.

"It was neck and neck until the fourth quarter when one of the Landry boys, I think it was Irvin, got loose on a 50-yard scamper. They scored with two minutes to play. We had a tough time getting out of there. Boy, that Livonia crowd, they hated to lose."

Although it might seem that military training and combat experience was an essential requirement for the six-man referees of the time, the referees seemed to relish their time officiating.

Gerald Didier says, "It was a great experience. It helped me in life and business. It showed me teamwork. After a hard week in business, I found it was a great way to relax. I am real happy that I was involved all those years."

The General concurs.

"I loved it. Did it for about 20 years. It was absolutely great to be out there. It really was a momentous part of my life, I'll never forget it. My wife came with me most of the time and she enjoyed it just as much as I did. It was great to be out there with the kids and, yes, even the crowd."

All joking aside, if military experience really had been a requirement to referee a six-man game in Louisiana, there'd be no shortage of candidates to choose from. In fact, Pointe Coupee Parish has a remarkable military record.

Pointe Coupee resident General John A. Lejeune was the 13th Commandant US Marine Corps and known as the greatest of all Leathernecks. General Robert Hilliard Barrow, the 27th Commandant of the US Marine Corps, was from across the bridge in West Feliciana Parish. General Dabadie and his son, Major General Stephen Dabadie are from Pointe Coupee. General deLesseps "Chep" Morrison, Mayor of New Orleans from 1946-61, was also a Brigadier-General as was Lt General Russel L. Honore.

It's not just decorated high-ranking officers that represent military accomplishment in the area.

General Dabadie says, "We've had more Second LTs in the infantry than any other small town. I could offhand name ten guys who were combat infantry in the European Theater of Operations that are highly decorated with Silver Stars, Distinguished Service Crosses, and Purple Hearts. Some fought in the Pacific. All came up through LSU ROTC. Pointe Coupee is abundant with combat line officers from WWII especially."

If you've read this book, you won't be surprised about the area's military accomplishments and accolades. The era in general and this area in particular, were characterized by hard work, strong values, family and community involvement, and dedicated service. So many people mentioned in this book made a huge difference to their communities and their country. They coached. They inspired. They taught. They led. They stepped in. They stepped up.

The coaches were an inspiration, literally transforming some of their students' lives. The wives and families of coaches were behind their husbands and fathers one hundred per cent and gladly accepted the life that goes with having a coach as a husband or a dad.

The Principals were revered, often giving decades of service and establishing and implementing a culture based on essential values. From Father DeBlanc to Miss Irene, these leaders influenced thousands of children for the betterment of the community, the country and, of course, the children themselves.

Six-man football was a reflection of difficult times, born as it was in tough economic circumstances that were ultimately transformed by the largest conflict ever seen. Six-man gave small communities not just a cause to celebrate but also a chance to draw closer together. But mostly, six-man was a mirror of the communities, reflecting back the values that defined a nation.

Coach makes peace with the refs — no flags! From left: Referee Alan "Buddy" LeBlanc, Coach Murphy, Referee Gerald Didier.

# More Pictures

1962-1963 Pride High School first six-man football team

Napoleonville High School 1947 - team record 6-4

Delcambre Panthers 1949-1950 – State runner-ups

Lake Arthur High School. Top, left to right: Clayton, Duhon, DeLaunay, Moore, Duhon, Hanks, oach Broussard. Middle: Comeaux, Benoit, Barilleau, Chapman, Broussard, Nunez. Bottom: Hoffpauir, Roy, Jordan, Armentor, Hanks.

1958 Chesbrough High School. H. Hyde, A. Westmoreland, C. Wall, L. Johnson, D. Lea, W. Cox, N. Varnado, J. Carrier, P. Graham, M. Bounds, G. Dess, R. Wiggins, L. Bounds, B. Hayden, P. Ballard, W. Ballard, Coach Joe Keller

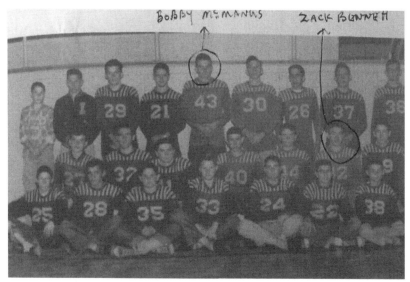

1952 Iota High School Bulldogs

1952 East-West All-Star football players

1948 Church Point High School – uncontested class A State Champions. First row, left to right: Russell Olivier, Howard Hargroder, Ronald Bellard, Richard Beaugh, Ray Francois, E.L. Melancon, Jerry Kirkpatrich, Bert Daigle. Bottom: Ed Daigle, Dale Capello, Bob McBride, Lester Harmon, Coach Willard Barnhill, Carl Andrus, Riley Beaugh, Manager Steward Bihm.

Iota High School mascots – Butch
McManus and Craig Bennett

1947 Clinton High School Eagles.

1947 Clinton High School cheerleaders. Top, left to right: Donald Howard, Eddie Clemmens. Bottom: Voncile Howard, Pat Bowles, Betty Jean McKay, Gay Marie Bolneke.

CHARLIE CLOUD, JR. MAMOU HIGH SIX-MAN FOOTBALL

RUNNING BACK. SCORED MOST POINTS IN SIX-MAN FOOTBALL
IN YEAR 1948. AVERAGE 21 Points each game

Future Brusly High School quarterback L.J. Dupuy (1958-1961) and brother Hubert

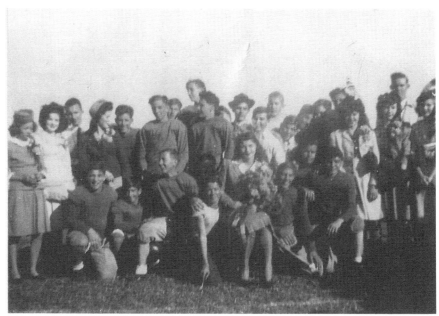

Rayne High School 1941 Homecoming Court

Livonia State Champions and Homecoming Queen

Livonia State Champions

1952 Iowa High School first six-man football team

Buddy Gilbert – All-State Fullback and Championship Team Co-Captain.
Entered the military in 1945 and played again at RHS in 1946, still being
eligible to play.

Miss Irene Petitjean

Former Dutchtown players and manager. Bottom, left to right:
Oscar (Rocky) Frederic, Lawrence LeBlanc, Owen Braud. Top:
Kermit Braud, B.F. Delaune, Elsey Webb, Red Nichols.

# About Coach Murphy

Coach Barrett Murphy has been a successful coach, strength and conditioning specialist, and media personality in a career that has spanned more than fifty years.

Coach Murphy has been successful at all facets of coaching; high school, collegiate and professional indoor football. He has variously been head coach, assistant coach, conditioning coach, and athletic director at numerous high schools, leading many to their first championships. He fulfilled defensive coach roles at both Nicholls State and McNeese State universities. He also established the annual state summer weight lifting league in the Baton Rouge area as well as introducing high school wrestling to east Baton Rouge Parish schools.

Coach Murphy proudly served in the Marine Corps from 1955-58.

In 1996 Coach Murphy was elected into the Louisiana Weight Lifting Hall of Fame in 1996. In 2009 he was elected into the Louisiana High School Athletic Association and the Louisiana High School Coaches Association Halls of Fame. He has also won Coach of the Year on several occasions and also received the "Super Sport" award for promoting high school athletics throughout the state of Louisiana in 1999.

Coach Murphy established the very popular high school radio show "The Friday Night High School Football Scoreboard" which has aired on radio in Baton Rouge and surrounding areas from the beginning of August through the state championship football game in December for the past twenty years.

Coach Murphy lives in Baton Rouge with Jennie, his wife for 55 years, and is the proud father of three children and grandfather of four grandchildren.

# Online

Coach Murphy encourages you to connect with him.

*Twitter* – @coach371

*Facebook* – Barrett Murphy

*LinkedIn*: Barrett Murphy

*Website:* www.louisianasixmanfootball.com

If you would like to book Coach Murphy for a presentation, keynote or book appearance, you can contact him at barrettmurphy@gmail.com.

Made in the USA
San Bernardino, CA
26 June 2014